Christoph Martin Wieland, Henry Christmas

The republic of fools

being the history of the state and people of Abdera, in Thrace

Christoph Martin Wieland, Henry Christmas

The republic of fools
being the history of the state and people of Abdera, in Thrace

ISBN/EAN: 9783741193637

Hergestellt in Europa, USA, Kanada, Australien, Japan

Cover: Foto ©Lupo / pixelio.de

Manufactured and distributed by brebook publishing software
(www.brebook.com)

Christoph Martin Wieland, Henry Christmas

The republic of fools

THE

REPUBLIC OF FOOLS.

THE

REPUBLIC OF FOOLS:

BEING

THE HISTORY

OF THE

STATE AND PEOPLE OF ABDERA,

IN THRACE.

Translated from the German of C. M. von Wieland,

BY

HENRY CHRISTMAS, M.A., F.R.S.,

ETC., ETC., ETC.

IN TWO VOLUMES.

VOL. I.

LONDON:

Wᴹ. H. ALLEN & CO., 7, LEADENHALL STREET

1861.

TO SIR EMERSON TENNENT, K.H.,

ETC., ETC., ETC.

MY DEAR SIR EMERSON,

"A Republic of Fools" needs a wise Protector; will you—especially gifted with that which the Abderites had not—accept the office of King Cassander? Permit me to subscribe myself,

Yours faithfully,

HENRY CHRISTMAS.

LONDON, *February*, 1861.

AUTHOR'S PREFACE.

THOSE who deem it necessary to ascertain for themselves the correctness of the principal facts and characteristic features of this history, may, unless they choose to have recourse to the original sources of information—viz. the works of Herodotus, Diogenes Laertius, Athenæus, Ælian, Plutarch, Lucian, Palæphatus, Cicero, Horace, Petronius, Juvenal, Valerius, Aulus Gellius, Solinus, &c., &c., turn to the articles "Abdera" and "Democritus" in Bayle's Dictionary; they will then see reason to believe that this history is not to be classed among those decided by Lucian to be true ones. The Abderites themselves, as well as their learned fellow-citizen Democritus, are here set in a correct light; and though the author, by supplying what was wanting, by clearing up what was obscure, by removing the real and reconciling the apparent contradictions found in the before-mentioned writers, may seem to have had access to narratives unknown to others, the intelligent reader will soon perceive that in all these things an authority has been followed whose support outweighs every testimony of Ælian and Plutarch, and against whose single voice the evidence of a whole world—of all the Amphyctyonics and Areopagites—Decemviri, Centumviri, Ducentumviri, of doctors, and masters, and bachelors, collectively and separately—is ineffectual—the voice of nature herself.

Should this little work be considered as a contribution, however small, to the history of the human understanding, the author will be well pleased. He thinks, however, that this high-sounding claim is neither more nor less than is made by every writer of history. He who should renounce it, would thereby reduce his works to the class of mere childish fables.

CONTENTS.

BOOK I.

DEMOCRITUS AMONG THE ABDERITES.

BOOK II.

HIPPOCRATES AMONG THE ABDERITES.

———

CHAPTER VIII.

CHAPTER IX.

CHAPTER X.

CHAPTER XI.

CHAPTER XII.

THE REPUBLIC OF FOOLS.

BOOK I.

DEMOCRITUS AMONG THE ABDERITES.

—◆—

CHAPTER I.

Preliminary observations on the origin of Abdera, and
the character of its inhabitants.

THE origin of the city of Abdera, in Thrace, is
lost in the remote antiquity of the heroic ages.
It is a matter of very little consequence at the
present time whether the name be derived from
Abdera, a sister of the renowned Diomedes,
whose love of horses* was so great, and his stud
so extensive, that they consumed both him and
his country; or from Abderus, his master of the
horse; or from another Abderus, a favourite of
Hercules.

* Palæphatus, in his treatise *De Incredib.*, thus explains
the fable that Diomedes fed his horses with human flesh,
and was at last thrown to them himself by Hercules.

It was many ages after its first foundation, and when Abdera was a heap of ruins, that Timesius, of Clazomenæ, undertook, about the 31st Olympiad, to rebuild it. The wild Thracians, who permitted no cities to spring up in their neighbourhood, allowed him no time to enjoy the fruits of his labour. They* soon drove him out, and the town remained unfinished and uninhabited till about the end of the 59th Olympiad.

At that period, the inhabitants of Teos, an Ionian city, unwilling to submit to the conquering arms of Cyrus, sailed to Thrace, and finding a city already built, in one of the most fruitful parts of that country, took possession of it as a forsaken and unappropriated territory. More successful than the builders, they made head against their Thracian neighbours; they and their successors assumed the name of Abderites, and founded a little state, which, like most Greek cities, was a mean between aristocracy and democracy, and was governed—as small republics ever have been.

And now, cry our readers, what is the object of this unmeaning deduction—the origin and fate of this little city, Abdera? What is Abdera to us, and of what moment is it to us whether

* Herodotus, i. 43.

we know, or whether we know not, when,
how, where, why, by whom, and to what end,
was built a town which for many centuries has
had no existence?

Patience, good reader, patience! till we (before
I go on further) are agreed in our requirements.
Heaven forbid that anybody should give himself
the trouble to read the History of the Abderites
if he has anything more necessary to do, or
anything better to read. "I must study my
sermon,"—"I must visit my patients,"—"I
have bought five yoke of oxen,"—"I have married a wife,"—then, in Heaven's name, study,
prescribe, plough, buy, and marry. Busy readers
are seldom good readers : sometimes one thing
distracts them, sometimes another; sometimes
they half understand us—sometimes not at all
—and sometimes (which is still worse) they mis-
understand us. He who would read with pleasure, or with profit, must have nothing else to
do—nothing else to think of. And if you are in
this condition, why should you not spend two or
three minutes to learn what has cost so many
hours to a Salmasius, to a Barnes, or to a Bayle,
and, to be candid, to me too, since I did not in
good time meet with the article in Bayle? Would
you not have patiently listened to me if I had

begun to relate to you the history of the king
in Bohemia who had seven castles, or the legend
of the three Calendars? Besides, the Abderites
should have been, according to what is said of
them, as refined, witty, lively, and intellectual a
people as ever the world beheld.

And why so?

This question will not probably be put by the
learned reader; but who would write books if
every reader knew as much as the author? The
question "Why?" is always a very reasonable
question; it deserves, in all conversations on
human affairs, an answer, and woe to him who is
embarrassed, or ashamed, or angry, when he is
required to give his opinion. We, for our part,
should have given ours unasked, had not the
reader been so impatient. Here it is. Teos
was an Athenian colony, one of the twelve, or
thirteen, planted in Ionia by Neleus, the son of
Codrus. The Athenians were ever a lively and
intellectual people. Travellers tell us they are
so still, and these Athenians settled in Ionia
advanced in mental powers, under the climate of
this favoured land, as the vine does in perfection
when transplanted into the south. The Ionian
Greeks were, above all nations of the earth, the
favourites of the Muses. Homer himself was,

according to all probability, an Ionian. The songs of love, the Milesian fables (the forerunners of our novels and romances), acknowledged Ionia for their native land. Alcæus, the Horace of the Greeks; the glowing Sappho; Anacreon, the songster; Aspasia, the preceptress; Apelles, the painter of the Graces—all were Ionians. Anacreon was a Teïan by birth. He was a youth of about eighteen years old when his countrymen removed to Abdera; he went with them, and as a proof that his lyre devoted to the Love-God was not left behind, there sang he that song to a Thracian maiden (in Barnes' edition the 61st)—a song in which the wild tones of the indomitable Thrace are mingled, and yet beautifully contrasted, with that Ionian grace so peculiar to his lyrics.

And now, who would not have supposed that the Teïans—in their first origin Athenians, so long established in Ionia, the fellow-citizens of an Anacreon—would have preserved, even in Thrace, the character of an intellectual people? The contrary, however, whatever may have been the reason of it, was without a doubt the case. Scarcely had the Teïans become Abderites when they began to degenerate: not that they altogether lost their former liveliness, and were changed

into sheep, as Juvenal asserts of them—their
liveliness merely took an extraordinary turn, and
their imagination stole so decided a march upon
their intellect, that they were never subsequently
able to recall it. The Abderites were not deficient in ideas, but their ideas seldom suited
the present occasion—they spoke much, but
ever without a moment's thought what they
should say, or how they should say it. The
natural consequence of this was, that they rarely
opened their mouths without giving utterance to
some folly. Unluckily this bad habit extended
itself to their deeds as well as their words, for
they commonly shut the cage when the bird
was flown. This drew upon them the reproach
of thoughtlessness, but experience proved that
they were none the better off when they did
think. Did any of their proceedings turn out
exceedingly stupid (a circumstance anything but
rare), the cause was sure to be that they wished
to do it too well; and if any state business gave
occasion to long and serious deliberation, it was
almost a matter of certainty that of all possible
decisions they would come to the very worst.
They became at last a proverb among the Greeks;
an Abderitish idea, an Abderitish trick, was
among them pretty much the same thing as a

Bull with us, or a Lalleburger among the Swiss; and the worthy Abderites failed not to furnish both jesters and laughers with a rich supply of subjects.

For the present, a few examples will do by way of proof. It once occurred to them that a city like Abdera ought to have a fine fountain. They decided that it should be in the centre of the market-place, and in order to defray the cost they laid on a new tax; a celebrated sculptor was sent for from Athens in order to prepare a group of statues representing the god of the sea in a chariot drawn by sea-horses, and surrounded by Nymphs, Tritons, and dolphins. It was intended that the sea-horses and dolphins should send forth *jets d'eau* from their nostrils. But when the work was completed, and the statues placed in the spot, it unfortunately appeared that there was scarcely water enough to wet the noses of the dolphins; and when the fountain was playing, both they and the horses had the uncomfortable appearance of being afflicted with a severe cold. In order to put a stop to the laugh, the group was brought into the temple of Neptune, and when exhibited to strangers the sacristan expressed his sorrow, in the name of the worshipful city of Abdera, that so rich and splendid a work of art was rendered useless by the poverty of nature. At another time they purchased a very lovely Venus, of ivory, which was reckoned among the masterpieces of Praxiteles. It was about five feet high, and ought to have been placed upon an altar of the goddess. As soon as it arrived, all Abdera fell into ecstasies about the beauty of their Venus; for the Abderites considered themselves acute connoisseurs and enthusiastic lovers of the arts. " She is too beautiful," exclaimed they with one voice, " to be placed on a low pedestal. A masterpiece that does our city so much honour, and which has cost us so much money, can scarcely be set too high; it should be the first thing that strikes the eye of the stranger on his entrance into Abdera." In consequence of this happy thought, they placed the small and exquisite statue upon an obelisk eighty feet in height; and as it was quite impossible at that distance to know whether it was a Venus or an oyster-wench, it became necessary to assure all strangers that nothing more perfect could be seen. These instances will be sufficient to prove that no injustice was done to the Abderites when they were characterized as blunderers; but it is doubtful whether any pro-

ceeding could display their character in a stronger
light than the following. According to the testimony of Justin, they allowed the frogs to increase
in and about their city to such an extent that they
were at last themselves obliged to give place to
their croaking fellow-citizens, and the result was,
that, under the protection of King Cassander, the
Abderites removed to another place. This misfortune did not fall upon them without warning.
A wise man who dwelt among them told them
long previously that this would finally be the
case. Indeed, the fault lay wholly in the means
they adopted to avoid the evil; only they could
not be induced to see this. What ought, however, to have opened their eyes was the fact that
they had not been many months removed from
Abdera when a number of cranes came down
from the regions of Gerania, and so completely
cleared away the frogs, that, for a mile round
Abdera, not one remained to greet the returning
spring with the chorus " κοαξ, κοαξ."

CHAPTER II.

Democritus of Abdera.—The question examined whether the native city of that eminent man could claim any share in his greatness, and, if so, how much.

No air, says Juvenal, is so thick, no nation so stupid, no place so unknown to fame, but that sometimes a great man arises to reflect lustre upon it. Pindar and Epaminondas were born in Bœotia, Aristotle in Stagyra, Cicero at Arpinum, Virgil in the village of Andes near Mantua, Albertus Magnus at Lessingen, Martin Luther at Eisleben, Sextus V. in the hamlet of Montalto in the marshes of Ancona, an'd one of the best kings that ever lived at Pau in Bearn : what wonder, then, that even Abdera should have the honour to give birth to the greatest naturalist of antiquity—Democritus ? For my part I do not see how a place can in itself add to or detract from the reputation of any great man, as, for every one who comes into this world, a birthplace must be found. It may be doubted whether, save Lycurgus, there was ever a legislator who extended his care and precaution to the Homunculus, in order to provide the state with fine, spirited, and well-organized children. We must confess that in this respect Sparta had some claim to the distinction which was shown to her citizens; but in Abdera (as in the whole world besides) chance and genius are permitted to decide.

Natale comes qui temperat astrum; and when a Protagoras* or Democritus arose amongst them, the good citizens of Abdera were as ignorant of the circumstance as were Lycurgus and his laws when a fool or a coward chanced to be born in Sparta.

But this indifference, though it might be said to concern a very important matter, must yet be allowed to pass, because nature, when left to herself, generally renders all extra care for the success of her works superfluous. But although she rarely forgets to endow her favourites with all those qualities by which accomplished men are

---

* A celebrated sophist of Abdera (somewhat earlier than the time of Democritus), whom Cicero ranks with Hippias, Prodicus, Georgias, and the greatest men of his profession.

distinguished, still education—the drawing out and developing of those qualities—is exactly the task which she leaves to art, and therefore every state must seek for itself the opportunity of affording that instruction which its citizens require. In this, however, the Abderites manifested great want of wisdom, and it would be difficult to find a place where less care was bestowed upon the cultivation of the intellect, the understanding, and the hearts of the citizens.

The formation of the taste arises from a keen and true perception of the beautiful, and is the best groundwork of the celebrated " Kalokagathia" of Socrates, making internal beauty and goodness of soul to constitute the noble-minded, beneficent, and happy man; and nothing is easier than to form in us this correct feeling of beauty, if all that we see and hear from our childhood be beautiful. It is no small advantage to be born in a place where the arts and the sciences are cultivated in the greatest perfection—in a well-built town filled with masterpieces of art, as in Athens ; and if, in the times of Plato and Menander, the Athenians had a thousand times more taste than other nations, they were doubtless in a great degree indebted to their native city for the advantage.

We have already stated* that the Abderites were enthusiastic in their love of the fine arts, and, indeed, at the time of their greatest splendour, when they were compelled to make way for the frogs, their town was filled with splendid buildings, rich in pictures and statues, provided with a fine theatre and music-hall, was, in short, a little Athens, in all save taste; but unfortunately the strong bias of which we have before spoken extended to their notions of the beautiful and becoming. Latona, the tutelary goddess of their town, had the worst temple; Jason, chief of the Argonauts (whose golden fleece they pretended to possess), the most splendid. Their town-hall looked like a warehouse, and immediately in front of the structure where the business of the state was transacted, cabbage-vendors, fruit and butter women, exposed their stores : on the contrary, the gymnasium, where their young men practised fighting and wrestling, was built upon three rows of columns, and the fighting hall was adorned with representations of deliberate assemblies, and statues in attitudes of grief or of

* Abdera, according to a Greek proverb (upon which, however, according to custom, the learned are not agreed), took the same name as does Florence in the Italian States, " the Beautiful."

thoughtful repose;* instead of these, within the senate-house was presented a more attractive and exciting spectacle, for in its halls the eyes of the senators frequently wandered to the surrounding objects, dwelling with delight on the conspicuously placed paintings of athletic champions, of Diana bathing, of sleeping Bacchantes, or Venus entangled in Olympus with one of her lovers in the net of Vulcan. This latter picture (immense in its proportions) was hung immediately over the benches of the most learned senators, and was always triumphantly pointed out to strangers as a *chef d'œuvre*. Even Phocion himself, grave as he was, would have been compelled, though it were the only time in his life, to indulge in a laugh. It is said King Lysimachus once offered six cities and a dominion of many leagues around them for this picture; but the Abderites could not make up their mind to part with so magnificent a piece, especially as it just filled the entire

---

* What is here said of the Abderites is by other ancient writers related also of the town of Alabanda.— *S. Cod. Rhodog. Lect. Ant.* lxxvi. cap. 25. [A similar example is to be seen in the present day at Naples, where the principal court of justice in the Vicaria is adorned by a picture of Naples given up to fire and sword by a conqueror!—TRANSLATOR.]

side of the court chamber, and, besides, one of the most celebrated critics had in a learned work suggested the connection of this allegorical painting with the place which it adorned.

To relate all the absurdities of this wonderful people would indeed be endless. One, however, we must not pass over, forming as it did a prominent feature of their constitution, and exercising no small influence over the character of the Abderites.

In the earliest periods of this city there was probably an institution in honour of Orpheus; and the nomophylax, or protector of the laws (one of the chief magistrates), was also leader of their sacred choruses, and precentor of their music in general. At this epoch there was good reason for that regulation; but length of time alone will cause great revolutions, and the observance of ancient laws would become ridiculous, if not modified according to changing circumstances: such a reflection, however, never entered the minds of the poor Abderites. It often happened that a nomophylax was chosen who tolerably well understood the laws, but who sang badly, or knew nothing at all of music. In such circumstances how managed the Abderites? After much and grave deliberation they resolved to

adopt the regulation that the best singer of
Abdera should in future be chosen for nomophylax, which rule was observed so long as Abdera
existed. That their nomophylax and their precentor might be two distinct personages was
never dreamt of, although they had twenty
public meetings on the subject.

It is easy to imagine that at this period music
was much esteemed in Abdera; everybody in
the city was musical—all sang and played on
the flute and lyre. Their ethics and politics,
their theology and cosmography, had each and
all a musical foundation ; nay, even their physicians cured their patients by harmonies and
melodies.

As far as speculation, mere theory, was
concerned, so far they seemed to attain to
much the same position as that of the greatest
sages of antiquity, of Orpheus, of Pythagoras,
and of Plato. But it unfortunately happened
that in practice they deviated all the more
decidedly from the severity of the rules they
professed.

Plato forbade all soft and effeminate strains in
his Republic. Music was meant to awaken in
the minds of his citizens neither joy nor grief,
and together with the Ionian and Lydian mea-

sures* he forbade all Bacchanalian ditties and love-songs, he prohibited the use of all sweet-toned instruments, as the many-stringed lute and the Lydian flute, as calculated to induce pernicious and sensual feelings; the citizens, however, were allowed the use of the guitar and the lyre, and the country people had the shepherd's reed or the pandean pipes. Philosophical enactments similar to these would have produced great dissatisfaction among the Abderites, who never restricted themselves from enjoying all the harmony afforded by their country. They endeavoured to do full justice to a very true, but unhappily by them much misunderstood maxim, that "all serious matters should be treated in a mirthful spirit, and all mirthful matters in a serious one." Extending this principle to music, they came to the most extraordinary conclusions—their sacred hymns sounded like drinking catches, but nobody ever heard strains more solemn than their dance music. The chorus of their tragedies was irresistibly comic, while their war-songs seemed only a fit accompaniment for a procession to the gallows; a performance on the lyre was only esteemed as it succeeded in imitating the flute, and a songstress who wished

* Plato *De Repub.* h. I. iii. Tom. opp. II., p. 398.

to gain admiration was obliged to warble and quaver like a nightingale.* The Abderites had no conception of music that excited the feelings of the heart, but were well satisfied if their ears only were pleased, and they would, without the slightest notice, interrupt the flow of the fullest and richest harmony. In one word, with all their enthusiasm for the arts, the Abderites had no taste, and it was all the same to them whether that which they deemed beautiful was esteemed so on just grounds or not; nature, chance, and good-luck, even when they combined their forces, could scarcely ever attain to so great a power of wonder-working as to endow a born Abderite with common sense. At least it must be allowed that if such a thing ever did happen, Abdera had done nothing towards it, for an Abderite was in general only so far a sensible man as he was destitute of all that marked him as an Abderite. This circumstance explains easily enough how it was that the Abderites esteemed the least those very citizens whom all foreigners regarded as doing their state the most honour. This was not one of their common-place absurdities; they had a reason for it, and

* Is this notion quite extinct among ourselves?—Let the frequenters of the Italian Opera decide.

one so natural that it would be unfair to reproach
them with it.   This reason was not, as some
suppose, because they had seen the naturalist
Democritus, for instance, before he became a
great man, or indeed a man at all, amuse himself by trundling a hoop, or by turning head
over heels on the grass.   Neither was it because,
either from spite or jealousy, they could not bear
the idea of a greater man being among them
than themselves.   As to the infallible inscription
over the Delphic Temple, not one of their number
had wisdom to penetrate its meaning, or from
that moment he would have ceased to be an
Abderite.   The true reason, my friends, why
the Abderites did not make much of their fellow-
citizen, Democritus, was, they did not esteem
him to be a wise man.

" And why not ? "

Because they could not.

" And why could they not ? "

Because in such a case they must have confessed themselves fools ; and that, at least, they
were not absurd enough to do.   In short, they
could with about as much ease have danced
upon their heads, taken the moon between their
teeth, or squared a circle, as they could have
comprehended one who was in all respects their

opposite; thus exemplifying a quality of human nature which must have been noticed even in the time of Adam. Helvetius gathered from this——never mind: what he deduced was thought quite new in his own day to many, but would now be deemed no novelty at all, and lost sight of every moment in consequence.

CHAPTER III.

What kind of man Democritus was.—His travels.—He
returns to Abdera.—What he brought with him, and
how he was received.—Undergoes an examination,
which serves as an example of Abderitan conversation.

DEMOCRITUS (I do not think the reader will
regret his time and trouble in making a further
acquaintance with the man) was above twenty
years of age when he inherited the possessions
of his father, one of the richest citizens of
Abdera. Instead of reflecting on the manner in
which he was to increase or to retain his fortune,
the young man resolved to make it the means of
self-improvement, by enriching and cultivating
his mind to the highest degree possible.

And what did the Abderites say to this resolution of the young Democritus?

The good people had never dreamed that the
mind could have any other interests than the
mouth, the stomach, and those other portions of

the animal economy which go to make up the whole visible man ; consequently they were not a little astonished at the wonderful freak conceived by their young countryman. For this, however, he cared nothing, but went forth on his way, and for his instruction employed many years in travelling through all such countries and islands as were then accessible. At that period persons anxious to obtain knowledge could only acquire it by personal observation : there were no printing-presses, no newspapers, libraries, magazines, encyclopædias, lexicons, royal dictionaries, or any other of the approved means whereby a man may now, without knowing how, become a philosopher, a critic, an author, in short a universal genius. At that time wisdom could only be attained at the expense of the most costly sacrifices—Lais herself was not more expensive. It was not every man who could go to Corinth, and consequently the number of learned men was small; but then, the knowledge they possessed was of an order all the higher.

Democritus did not merely travel as did Ulysses, to ascertain the customs and constitutions of mankind—nor as Plato, to seek after priests and visionaries—nor like Pausanias, to gaze on temples, statues, pictures, and objects of

archæology—neither like Dr. Solander, to identify
and classify plants and animals; but he journeyed
to explore the beauties of nature and art in all
their effects and causes, and especially to study
man in every state—rude or polished, ingenuous
or deceitful, perfect or imperfect—and whatsoever
besides might aid him in thoroughly understanding human nature. " Caterpillars," said Democritus, " in Ethiopia, are surely but caterpillars.
But what is a caterpillar?—is it so important as
to become a primary study for man ? Well, now
we are here, we will among other objects study
the caterpillars of Ethiopia. There is a worm in
the land of Seres which produces clothes and
maintains a million of human beings : who
knows whether the same useful caterpillar might
not be found on the banks of the Niger?"
Through this mode of thinking and reflecting,
Democritus collected in his travels a fund of
knowledge which to him was more valuable
than all the gold in the treasury of an Eastern
monarch, or the pearls which adorned the arms
and necks of his consorts. His knowledge
extended from the cedar of Lebanon to the mite
in an Arcadian cheese—running through an infinite variety of trees, shrubs, vegetables, grasses,
and mosses—and was conversant not merely with

their formation, names, and genus; but also with their properties, powers, and virtues. But what he appreciated a thousand times more than all his other knowledge was, that at the different places where he thought it worth his while to stop, he had become acquainted, during his sojourn, with the wisest and best men. It soon became evident that he was one after their own heart; they became his friends, and in the course of conversation they spared him many years of what might have been fruitless toil, by imparting to him the results of their own experience, their own diligence, or their own good fortune.

When, after an absence of twenty years, Democritus, enriched in mind and heart, returned to Abdera, his countrymen had almost forgotten him. He was become a stately and dignified man, courteous and polite, demeaning himself as a man of the world, who had gained much wisdom from mixing with his fellow-creatures; his complexion, slightly bronzed, told that he had come from the ends of the world, and he had brought with him a stuffed crocodile, a live monkey, with many other wonderful things. For some days the Abderites talked of nothing but their fellow-citizen Democritus, who had returned home with such curiosities; but after

a short time they began to think they had perhaps rather overrated the great traveller. The
worthy person to whose care Democritus had
intrusted his estate, had evidently robbed him
of at least half his revenues; yet the naturalist,
without hesitation, passed all his accounts. It
was but natural that such a proceeding as this
should give a great shock to that notion of his
wisdom which his countrymen had begun already
to entertain; the barristers and attorneys, who
had reasonably looked forward to some pretty
pickings by way of law-suits, now shrugged
their shoulders, and uniformly expressed their
opinion, that a man who had so little sense of
his own private interests was obviously unfit to
be intrusted with those of the republic. In
the mean time, the Abderites did not doubt
that he would speedily become a candidate for
some high and honourable public employment.
Accordingly they began to calculate at what
price they might sell him their votes; one offered
him a daughter, another a grandchild, a sister-
in-law, or aunt, in marriage, estimating the ad-
vantages they might derive from his influence
when he should become their chief magistrate,
priest of Latona, &c.

Democritus, however, declared that he had no

wish to become a common-councilman in Abdera,
or to marry an Abderite lady. Although this
resolution frustrated all such plans, they yet
hoped to profit, in some way or other, by his
acquaintance and conversation : a man who had
brought with him from his travels an ape, a
crocodile, and a tame dragon, must have many
wonderful adventures to relate. They expected
he would tell them of giants twelve yards, and
of dwarfs six inches high, of men with dogs'
and asses' heads, of mermaids with green hair,
of white negroes, and of blue Centaurs. But
Democritus lied little, and indeed less than if
he had never crossed the Thracian Bosphorus.

They asked him whether in the country of
the Garamantes he had not met with people
without heads, and having their eyes, noses,
and mouths upon their breasts ; and an extremely wise scholar, who, though he had
never been beyond the walls of his native
city, gave himself such airs as though there was
not a hole in the earth that he had not crept
through, intimated his opinion to a large company, that Democritus had either never been
to Ethiopia, or must, when there, have necessarily made acquaintance with the Agriophagæ,
whose king had only one eye, placed exactly over

his nose ; with the Ptœambatœ, who.always chose a dog for their king ; or with the Artabatites, who go on all fours ; *—" and if you have penetrated into the extreme part of Western Ethiopia," continued the learned man, " I am certain that you must have encountered a people without noses, and another part where the inhabitants have such small mouths that they are compelled to take their soup through a tube of straw."†

Democritus protested by Castor and Pollux that he could not remember ever having had the honour of meeting with such. " At least," said the questioner, " you met in India with people born with only one leg, but who, notwithstanding, in consequence of the extraordinary breadth of their foot, glide over the ground so quickly that a man on horseback can scarcely keep pace with them ; ‡ what can you say to that ? Did you not also, at the source of the Ganges, meet with a people whose sole nutriment was the scent of wild apples ? § "

* Pliny's Nat. Hist., B. 4.

† Solinus, B. 30, also Pliny, Mela Pomponius, and other ancient and modern writers, who unhesitatingly speak of such wonderful creatures as though they really existed.

‡ Solinus Polyhistor.

§ Idem.

"Oh! do tell us all about it," cried out eagerly the Abderite ladies, "do tell us, Mr. Democritus. What could you not tell us if only you would!"

Democritus swore, but to no purpose, that neither in India nor Ethiopia had he seen or heard of such wonderful creatures. "Well, what have you seen, then?" asked a round, short personage, who was indeed neither one-eyed like the Agriophagæ, nor dog-headed like the Cynomolgi; neither did he carry his eye on his shoulder like an Omophthalmian; neither, from the simple act of inhaling odour, did he subsist like the bird of Paradise. Notwithstanding all this, he had no more brains in his skull than an American humming-bird, but was none the less qualified for being a town-councillor of Abdera. "Well! but what have you seen?" said the stout gentleman, "you who for twenty years have been travelling about the world, and have seen nothing of all these things. What else can you have seen that is wonderful in those distant countries?"

"Wonderful!" replied Democritus, smiling; "I really found my time so much occupied in examining that which was natural, that I had none to spare for the merely wonderful."

"I must confess," said the stout gentleman, "that it does not repay one for the fatigue of passing over so many seas, and ascending so many high mountains, not to see more than one of us can see just as well at home."

Democritus did not like to quarrel with people about their opinions, and least of all with the Abderites, yet he was unwilling they should suppose that after all his travels he had absolutely nothing to say; he therefore endeavoured to choose from among the fair Abderites who were of the party, one to whom he could unreservedly explain all he had to tell. He fixed on one with the eyes of a Juno, which, in spite of his great experience, led him erroneously to suppose that their owner possessed a little more intellect and perception than the rest.

"What could I do," said he to her, "with a lady whose eye was placed on her forehead or on her elbow? or how would all my knowledge of art help me to awaken the heart of a cannibal beauty? Besides, I have always been too well satisfied with the soft influence of two fine eyes placed in their natural position, to be tempted to look tenderly on the great ox-eye of a female Cyclops."

The beauty with the large eyes was doubtful

how to understand this speech, and gazed at the speaker with silent astonishment, smiled, displayed her fine teeth, and then looked from side to side, as though endeavouring to penetrate his meaning.

The other ladies had understood it as little as she did, but because Democritus had addressed himself to this one with the large eyes, they decided that he had said something very agreeable to her, and this they signified to each other by a variety of grimaces; one wrinkled up her little nose, another pursed up her mouth, a third distended hers, which was already large enough, a fourth opened widely her little eyes, a fifth drew herself up to her full height, and Democritus saw all this, remembered he was in Abdera, and—was silent.

CHAPTER IV.

The examination is continued, and turns upon a dispute as to beauty, in which Democritus becomes much excited.

To be silent is sometimes an art, yet not so great a one as certain people would have us believe, who are wisest when they are most silent.

If a wise man finds himself in the company of children, he has only to act accordingly, and talk to them in their own way.

" I have been, indeed," said Democritus to his inquisitive companions, " candid enough to confess that of all those things about which you have questioned me I have seen none; but do not imagine that in my various travels by sea and land, I have not noticed many things which might gratify your curiosity. Believe me, they are things that would appear to you much more wonderful than any of those of which you have been speaking."

At these words the fair Abderites opened both eyes and ears, and drew nearer.

"That is a speech worthy of a traveller," said the corpulent alderman, while the scholar elevated his eyebrows, hoping he should find something or other to criticize or improve upon, let Democritus say what he might.

"I was once in a country," began Democritus, "where I was so well pleased that, during the first three or four days I spent there, I wished myself immortal, that I might remain there for ever."

"I never left Abdera," said the alderman, "but I believe that there is not another place in the world that I should prefer to it; and I feel the same here as you did in the country with which you were so much pleased. I would with pleasure resign all the rest of the world could I but be immortal and remain for ever here. But what was the reason that you were so delighted with the country after only a three days' residence?"

"You shall hear presently. Imagine a vast country, most charmingly varied by hills, valleys, forests, mountains, and meadows; under the dominion of perpetual spring 'and autumn, every spot cultivated and irrigated, everywhere blooming and fruitful, always verdant; abounding with forests of the finest fruit trees,—grapes, figs, lemons, and pomegranates, growing spontaneously like the oaks in Thrace,—groves of myrtle and jasmine, the flowers beloved by Eros and Cytheræa, not in hedges as in this our country, but in dense tufts and large trees, and as full blown as my lovely countrywomen." (This was rather a mistake of Democritus, and it may serve as a caution to future narrators that it is better to look at the society they are amongst before paying such compliments, however flattering they may sound.) The beauties placed their hands before their eyes and blushed, because unfortunately there was not one among them who could do honour to the comparison, although they did not fail to puff themselves out as well as they could.

"And these delightful groves," he continued, "were animated by the song of innumerable birds, and filled with myriads of many-coloured parrots, eclipsing the splendour of the sun with their varied hues. What a country! I cannot conceive why the Goddess of Love has chosen Cythera for her residence, when a spot like this exists in the world. Where could the Graces more pleasantly join in the dance than in the country where the groves wave deliciously over the banks of transparent violets and sparkling springs, and where, in the midst of a dense verdure of the liveliest green, lilies and hyacinths, with a thousand other beautiful flowers whose names are unknown to us, are blooming naturally, and filling the air with luxurious fragrance?"

It is easy to suppose that the ladies of Abdera had not less lively imaginations than the men, and the picture which Democritus, without intending any harm, had so vividly drawn, was more than their weak minds could support; some sighed with delight, some looked as if they could inhale even there those voluptuous perfumes; the beautiful Juno let fall her head on the cushion of the sofa, half shut her magnificent eyes, and fancied herself transported to the blooming borders of one of those springs shaded by roses and citron trees, from the branches of which clouds of ambrosial vapour greeted her. She began, in the midst of that sweet sensation, to slumber, and then she thought she beheld kneeling before her a youth beautiful as the son of Semele, importunate as Love himself; she rose to contemplate him better, and found him so graceful and glorious that the words with which she was about to reprove him——— Scarcely had she———

" And what do you think is the name of this fairy country of which all I could say would give you but a shadowy notion ? It is just that very Ethiopia which, by my learned friend, is accounted so populous in human monsters, certainly, very unworthy natives of such a fatherland ; but I again repeat that in all Ethiopia or Libya, though those countries contain so many different nations, there is not a man to be seen who carries his head otherwise than we do, or who has not just as many eyes and ears as ourselves, and in a word———"

A heavy sigh which might proceed from a heart oppressed either by pain or pleasure, issued at this moment from the bosom of the beautiful Abderite, who, during the time of the narration of Democritus, dreamed all the particulars in which her heart took so deep an interest ; but as none around her could be aware that in her reverie she had fancied herself some hundreds of miles from Abdera, in the midst of the sweetest odours, listening to a thousand birds trilling their love-songs, and viewing the countless parrots with their variegated plumage, and above all that she had imagined a handsome youth with golden locks and coral lips kneeling at her feet, who could be surprised that this sigh was heard with general astonishment?

" What is the matter with you, Lysandra ? " unanimously exclaimed the ladies, anxiously surrounding her.   The fair Lysandra, who at once perceived where she was, blushed and assured them it was nothing.   Democritus, becoming aware what was the real state of the case, persuaded them that a draught of fresh air would quickly restore her ; but he mentally determined in future to paint all his pictures of one colour only, as was the custom in Thrace.

" Ye gods ! " thought he, " what excitable imaginations do these Abderite women possess !"

" Well, my fair inquisitive countrywomen," continued Democritus, " what do you think is the colour of the inhabitants of this beautiful country ? "

" What colour ! why should they be of a different colour from other people?   Did you not tell us that their noses were in the middle of their faces, and that in every other respect they were the same kind of beings as we Greeks are ? "

" Undoubtedly ; but would they be the less

men and women if they were born of a darker hue ? "

" What do you mean ? "

" I mean that the handsomest among the Ethiopian nations (that is to say, those who, according to our ideas of beauty, resemble us the most) are those of a brown or olive complexion, as the Egyptians ; and those who live further on, in the more southern parts, are, from the crown of their head to the sole of their foot, as black as the ravens of Abdera."

" Is it possible? And don't the people scream out at one another when they meet ? "

" Scream ! for what reason ? They please each other with their raven blackness, and fancy that nothing can be more charming."

" How droll ! " cried the Abderites, " to be as black as if they had been dipped in pitch, and then dream of beauty—how stupid must such people be ! Have they no painters to depict them an Apollo, a Bacchus, or the Goddess of Love and the Graces ? Or can they not learn from Homer that Juno had white arms, Thetis silver feet, and Aurora rosy fingers ? "

" Oh ! " replied Democritus, " these good people have no Homer; or if they have one, depend upon it that his Juno will have arms as black as coals. I have heard nothing of painters in Ethiopia, but I saw a girl whose beauty had occasioned as much mischief among her countrymen as the daughter of Leda among the Greeks and Trojans, and this African Helen was as black as ebony."

" Oh, describe to us this marvellous beauty! " cried the fair Abderites, who, from the most natural cause in the world, took the greatest interest in the recital.

"You will have some difficulty in forming a notion of it. Imagine the complete reverse of what a Greek considers as beauty ; the elegance of a Grace, and the plenitude of a Ceres ; imagine black hair, not flowing in curls on the shoulders, but short, and naturally frizzled, like wool ; the forehead wide and incurvated ; the nose short, slit in the middle, and the gristle squeezed flat ; the cheeks round, like those of a trumpeter ; the mouth"—(here Philena smiled in order to show how small her own was)—"the lips very thick and turned upwards, and two rows of teeth like strings of pearls."

The beauties laughed all at once, although they could have no reason for so doing but to display their teeth—for what was there to laugh at ?

" But their eyes ? " asked Lysandra.

" Oh ! as to her eyes, they were so small and so watery that it was long before I could consider them pretty."

" Democritus approves of Homer's ox-eyes, it seems," said Myris, looking ironically at the large-eyed beauty.

"In fact," replied Democritus, with a look from which the most innocent mind might have concluded that he was disposed to flatter, " beautiful eyes cannot be too large, nor ugly ones too small."

The lovely Lysandra cast a glance of triumph upon her sisters, and her large eyes shed forth a whole glory of delight upon the happy Democritus.

"May I ask what you mean by beautiful eyes ?" asked the little Myris, and her nose seemed perceptibly to sharpen.

A glance from the fair Lysandra seemed to tell him, " You certainly will not be embarrassed to find an answer to this question."

" I mean the eyes through which shines a high and noble soul," said Democritus.

Lysandra looked perfectly disconcerted, as one who had heard something quite unexpected, and was at a loss for a reply. " A beautiful soul !"

thought the fair Abderites; "what strange notions the man has brought out of foreign countries! This beats his monkeys and parrots."

" But a truce to these subtleties," said the sleek alderman. " I think we were speaking of the fair Helen of Ethiopia; and I should be very glad to learn what intelligent people could find pretty in her."

" Everything!" replied Democritus.

" Then they can have no idea of beauty," said the learned man.

" Pardon me," replied the narrator; " but as this Ethiopian Helen was the object of the admiration and the desire of all, it must be concluded that she accorded with the idea of beauty which each one among them found in his own imagination."

" You are of the school of Parmenides? Parmenides of Elis is recognized as the inventor of the doctrine of ideas or essential images; it was received by Plato into his system, and, being so appropriated, is generally called by his name," said the scholar, putting himself in an argumentative posture.

" I am nothing but myself, which is very little," replied Democritus, half frightened. " If you are adverse to the word *idea,* let me express

myself in another way. The beautiful Gulleru
(this is the name of the negress of whom we
are speaking)——"

" Gulleru!" exclaimed the ladies, bursting
into a laugh which threatened to be interminable
—" what a name!"

" And what became of your beautiful Gulleru?"
asked the sharp-nosed Myris, with a look and
tone three times as sharp as her nose.

" If you ever honour me with a visit," replied
the philosopher, with the utmost courtesy, "you
will learn what is become of the beautiful
Gulleru. Now I must keep my promise to these
gentlemen. The figure of the beautiful Gulleru——"

" The beautiful Gulleru!" repeated the ladies
again, with another burst of Abderitan laughter;
but this time Democritus did not suffer himself
to be interrupted. He continued : " —unluckily
inspired the young men of her country with the
deepest passion. This seems to prove that she
was deemed pretty; and without doubt the
reason that she was thought so beautiful was the
same as that for which she was not deemed ugly.
These Ethiopians understood the difference between what was pretty and otherwise; and if
they agreed in their judgment upon this Helen,

it must have been because they were unanimous in their idea of beauty and ugliness."

" It is not a consequence," said the learned Abderite ; " might not each find something different and peculiarly lovely in her ?"

" That is not impossible, but proves nothing against my argument. Agreed that one may have admired her little eyes, another her thick lips, a third her large ears, then this supposes a comparison between her and the other Ethiopian beauties. The others had eyes, lips, and ears, just as Gulleru: if hers were found prettier than common, then they formed a model of beauty in which, for instance, her eyes might be compared with other eyes, and so on ; and this is all I meant by my ideal image."

" However," replied the learned man, " you will not pretend to affirm that this Gulleru was unquestionably the prettiest among all black girls before, in, and after, her own time,—I mean the prettiest in comparison with the model you have been speaking of."

" I cannot see why I should affirm it," replied Democritus.

" There might be another, having, for instance, smaller eyes, thicker lips, larger ears ?"

" Possibly, for aught I know."

"And in reference to this last the same presumption may serve, and so on without end, so that the Ethiopians could have no model of beauty; for must it be said that endless eyes, endless lips, and endless ears, can be supposed?

"How subtle the learned men in Abdera are!" thought Democritus. "When I admitted that there might be a black girl with smaller eyes or thicker lips than Gulleru's, I did not say that she would be therefore more agreeable to the Ethiopians than Gulleru. Beauty must have a determined measure, and what is beyond this is removed as far from it as that which falls short. Who would conclude that the Greeks have ever imagined perfect beauty to consist in the largeness of the eyes or the smallness of the mouth, or that a lady whose eyes were two inches across, or whose mouth was too small to insert a straw in it, would therefore be esteemed by the Greeks as supremely beautiful?"

The Abderite was beaten, and it was clear that he felt it. But a learned Abderite would rather be choked than confess himself vanquished—were not Philena and Lysandra and the stout alderman there, whose good opinion he wished to obtain? And how easy it was for him to bring Abderite ladies and gentlemen to his side! For a moment he knew not what to say, but, in full confidence that a thought would come, he answered in the mean time with an ironical smile, which, as he thought, proved his contempt for the arguments of his opponent, and a readiness to strike the decisive blow.

"Is it possible?" he exclaimed at last, as if he were replying to the last speech of Democritus;* "can you carry your love of paradox so far as to affirm, in the presence of these beauties, that a creature like this Gulleru whom you have just described, was a Venus?"

"You have forgotten," replied Democritus quite composedly, "that we have not been speaking of myself and these beauties here present, but of Ethiopians. I did not affirm anything; I was simply relating what I have seen, and have described to you a beauty according to the Ethiopian taste. It is not my fault if the Greek ugliness be considered beauty in Ethiopia, nor can I see the right I have to decide between Greeks and Ethiopians—I presume it is possible that both are right."

A loud shout of laughter, such as is usually elicited elsewhere by a nonsensical speech,

* A very common trick of Abderite scholars and critics.

assailed the philosopher from every quarter. " Hear! hear!" cried the sleek alderman, holding his sides with both hands. " What *can* our countryman say to prove that both are right? I should like above all things to hear such an argument—for what other purposes are learned men? The earth is round—the snow black— the moon is ten times as large as the whole Peloponnesus—Achilles could not overcome a tortoise in the race! Is it not so, Mr. Antistrepsiades?—is it not, Mr. Democritus? You see that I too am a little initiated in your mysteries—ha! ha! ha!"

All the Abderite ladies and gentlemen again sympathized in his mirth; and Mr. Antistrepsiades, who had already made an attack upon the supper of the jovial alderman, had the politeness to support the general laughter with loud applause.

CHAPTER V.

Unexpected solution of the difficulty, with new examples of Abderitan wit.

DEMOCRITUS was in the humour to amuse himself with the Abderites, and they were equally willing to be amused with him; if he were too wise to criticize their national or individual faults, he was willing to be taken by them for an overwise man, whose native brilliance had become a little tarnished by travelling, and who was now only useful, by his whims and caprices, to afford them merriment. He continued, after the laughter caused by the witty conceit of the stout alderman had subsided, from the point where he had been interrupted by the jocose little man :—

"Did I not tell you that if the Greek ugliness could be esteemed beauty in Ethiopia, it might happen that both were right?"

"Yes, yes, you did say so; and a man is responsible for his words."

"If I said it, of course I must prove it; that is certain, Mr. Antistrepsiades."

"If you can."

"Am I not also an Abderite? and, besides, I have only to prove the half of my position in order to prove the whole. That the Greeks are right it is not necessary to prove,—this is a question which they themselves have long ago decided; but to prove that the Ethiopians are right too, there lies the difficulty. If I intended to fight my opponents with sophisms, or to rest satisfied by silencing without convincing them, I would, as the advocate of the Ethiopian Venus, leave the decision of the case to internal conviction. Why, would I say, do men fancy this or that figure or complexion beautiful? Because it pleases them very well."

"But wherefore is it pleasing?"

"Because it is agreeable to them."

"And why agreeable?"

"My dear sir, I would beg leave to say, you must cease to ask, or I cease to answer. A thing is agreeable to us because it makes an agreeable impression upon us. I challenge all your hypercritics to find another reason. Well,

it would be ridiculous to try to persuade a man
that the thing which he likes is unpleasant, or
that he is wrong in pleasing himself in a way
that he finds agreeable; consequently, if the
figure of a Gulleru most delights him, then she
most pleases him; and if she pleases, then he
calls her beautiful, or such a word is useless in
his language."

"And if an insane man eat stale eggs for
fresh ones," said Antistrepsiades, "what then?"

"Stale eggs for fresh ones! Well said, upon
my honour! Beat that, Mr. Democritus," exclaimed the alderman.

"Fie, fie! Democritus," whispered Myris,
holding her hand before her face; "how can
you speak of stale eggs? At least, spare our
noses."

Everybody may see that the lady ought to
have addressed this reproof to the wily Antistrepsiades, as he it was who first had mentioned the objectionable eggs, or to the alderman
who had proposed to Democritus to beat the
notion; but it was said with a view of making
Democritus appear ridiculous. Those present
agreed with Myris, who could not lose this
opportunity of raising the laugh on her side.
That Democritus should not only swallow the

eggs of Antistrepsiades, but also receive a reproof in addition, appeared so agreeable to these ladies and gentlemen, that they all laughed at once, and began to demean themselves as if the philosopher were entirely beaten and could not rally again.

One may carry a joke too far. The good-natured Democritus had experienced a great deal during the last twenty years, but since he left his native town, never had he met with a second Abdera; and now, being back again, he could for a moment scarcely realize where he was. What could he do?—how was he to deal with such people?

"Well, cousin," said the alderman, "so you cannot digest these eggs—ha! ha! ha!"

The ladies tittered "hi! hi! hi!" in a shriller tone, amidst the shouting of the gentlemen's "ha! ha! ha!"

"I am vanquished," cried Democritus, "and to prove that I take my defeat in good part, you shall see if I am deserving the honour to be your countryman and relative." He then began, with a skill in which no Abderite was his equal, to intone a laugh, from the lowest tone gradually ascending to the unisons of the "hi! hi! hi!" of the ladies; such a laugh was

never heard before nor after, while Abdera stood
on the ground of Thrace.

At first the ladies tried to resist, but it was
impossible to stand against the desperate cres-
cendo—they were at last carried away as by a
rapid current, and the power of contagion went
so far that the case appeared serious.   The
ladies asked mercy with weeping eyes, but Democritus turned a deaf ear, and the laugh in-
creased.   At last it seemed that he intended to
grant them a truce, but, in fact, only to enable
them to prolong the torture he intended them;
for scarcely had they recovered their breath
when he recommenced the same scale a note
higher, but running into so many shakes and
roulades that even the wrinkled judges, Minos,
Æacus, and Rhadamanthus, in their fiendish
court, would not have been able to keep their
countenance.   How much bright hair was
shaken out of curl, how many corsages irre-
mediably damaged, how many delicate sides
doomed to a month's aching, how many di-
gestions disturbed, and how many proprieties
disordered—who shall say?   To add to the
absurdity, in the midst of all this the stout
little alderman exclaimed that he would not ex-
change this evening for half Thrace, making the

scene worthy the pencil of a Hogarth, had a Hogarth then existed.

We cannot tell how long it might have lasted, because it was one of the peculiarities of the Abderites that they never knew when to leave off; but Democritus, with whom everything had its time, thought a comedy which never came to an end a very tedious pastime. He kept to himself all the pretty things which he could have said in defence of the Ethiopian Venus if he had had sensible beings to reason with, wished to all the ladies and gentlemen what they did not possess, and went home, not without feeling much astonishment at the society which might be found in that city by calling on an alderman.

CHAPTER VI.

An opportunity for the reader to recover his equanimity after the commotion caused by the events of the former chapter.

" Good, artless, simple-minded Gulleru !" said Democritus, on his return home, to a well-conditioned, curly-headed black woman, who came waddling towards him with open arms. "Come to my heart, honest Gulleru ! It is true you are black as the goddess of night, your hair is woolly and your nose is flat, your eyes are small and your ears are large, and your lips like a budding peony ; but your heart is pure, sincere, joyous, and kind. You think evil of no one, never practise deceit nor torment yourself with the affairs of others, and do nothing you would be ashamed to confess. Your soul is without falsehood, as your face is without paint ; you know neither envy nor mischievous joy, and never has your flat, honest nose been drawn

into a wrinkle by scoffing at a fellow-creature.
Whether you charm or not, is to you the same;
your life is innocent, at peace with yourself and
the whole world, always ready to please and
to be pleased, and deserving of man's trust
and affection. Good, gentle-hearted Gulleru!
I could give you another name, ending with
ane or *ide*, *arion* or *erion*; but your name is
pretty enough, because it is *yours*, and I am not
Democritus if the time is not coming when
every honest heart will respond to the name
of Gulleru."

Gulleru could not comprehend the meaning of
this sentimental speech of Democritus, but she
perceived that it was a literal outpouring of the
heart; and in this way she understood as much
as was necessary.

"Was this Gulleru his wife?"

"No."

"Was she his mistress?"

"No."

"Was she his slave?"

"To judge by her appearance, no."

"How then was she attired?"

"As handsomely as if she had been a maid of
honour to the Queen of (Sheba). Rows of
pearls ornamented her locks, her arms, and her

neck; a garment of fine stuff, with stripes of various colours richly draped, and confined round the waist by a splendidly embroidered girdle, closed by an emerald clasp; and what need I add more?"

"The attire was rich indeed."

"At least you may rest assured that as she appeared, no Prince of Senegal, Angola, Gambia, Congo, or Loango, could have beheld her with undazzled eyes."

"But——"

"I perceive that you have not yet arrived at the end of your questions. Who was this Gulleru? Was she the same who was spoken of before? How came she with Democritus, and on what footing was she living in his house? I own these are fair questions, but for the present I confess my inability to answer them. Do not think that I am unnecessarily reserved, or that there is any peculiar secresy in the matter. The reason why I cannot give you an answer is the most simple in the world. Thousands of authors have been in a similar position, but amongst them all, scarcely one would candidly confess the reason. Shall I explain to you mine? Well, in short, I know nothing whatever about it; and as I am not the historian of the beautiful Gulleru, you will understand that I am under no obligation respecting that lady. Should it happen (which I do not foresee) that an opportunity should occur of learning more particulars touching Democritus and her, depend upon it everything shall be made known to the reader."

CHAPTER VII.

Patriotism of the Abderites, their sympathy for Athens as their mother-city.—Some proofs of their Atticism, and of the unpleasant sincerity of the wise Democritus.

DEMOCRITUS had scarcely been a month amongst the Abderites when he became as insupportable to them, and the Abderites to him, as men can be to each other who disagree every moment in their ways of thinking and acting.

The Abderites entertained the highest opinion of themselves, their town, and republic. Their ignorance of every important event which had occurred out of their district, was at once the reason and the consequence of so ridiculous a notion. It therefore resulted, by a very natural train of reasoning, that they could not perceive how anything could be right and proper which was otherwise managed than in Abdera, or that was unknown to them. A notion at variance with their own ideas, a habit differing from

theirs, a manner of thinking or reasoning
which was new to them, was considered, without
further investigation, as ridiculous and absurd.
Even nature was repudiated in the narrow sphere
of their action, and although they went not so
far as the Japanese do, in believing that out of
their locality only devils, spectres, and monsters
were to be found, they regarded the other
portions of the globe, and its inhabitants, as
unworthy of their attention; and if accidentally
they found an opportunity of learning or seeing
anything new, they were puzzled what to do
except to wonder and congratulate themselves
that they were not like other people. This was
carried so far that they could not recognize a
good citizen in the man who had seen, in other
places, better customs and establishments than
at home. Whosoever would please them must
act and speak as if the town and government of
Abdera, with all it contained, were irreproach-
able, and the very *beau idéal* of a good republic.

The city of Athens alone was exempted from
this contempt of everything not Abderitan, but
this only because the Abderites looked up to it
as their mother-country. They were proud to
be acknowledged as the " Thracian Athens; "

and though this appellation was only given to
them ironically, they prided themselves on the
flattery, and endeavoured to imitate the Athenians in everything, copying them about as
justly as a monkey imitates a man. If, in order
to appear lively and spirited, they fell every
moment into the ridiculous;—if they treated
serious things with levity, and childish ones
seriously;—if they assembled the people or the
town-council twenty times upon every trifle, in
order to speak and listen to long speeches on
subjects that might be decided in a quarter of
an hour by any man of common sense;—if they
were continually projecting improvements and
enlargements, discovering as soon as they were
begun that it was beyond their means to complete them;—if they interlarded their half-
Thracian language with Athenian phrases;—if,
without the least taste, they affected a great
passion for the arts, and always talked of
pictures, statues, music, orators, and poets,
without having had one painter, sculptor, orator,
or poet, deserving to be so called;—if they
built temples like baths, and baths like temples;
—if they ordered the picture of the net of Vulcan for their town-hall, and that of the restitu-
tion of the lovely Chryseis for their academy;—

if they went to comedies which made them cry and to tragedies which made them laugh,—in these and a thousand other matters the good people fancied themselves Athenians, and were, in fact,—Abderites.

"How sublime and sonorous is the poem by Physignathus about my quail!" said an Abderite lady.

"So much the worse!" said Democritus.

"Look," said the archon of Abdera, "at that part of this building, which is intended for an arsenal. It is constructed of the finest Parian marble; confess that you never before saw so tasteful a work."

"It has certainly cost the republic a great deal of money," answered Democritus.

"That can never cost too much which does honour to the republic," replied the archon, feeling himself, at the moment, another Pericles.

"I know you are a connoisseur, Democritus, as you have always something to criticize in everything. Pray do find me a fault in this façade."

"A thousand drachmas for a defect, Mr. Democritus!" cried a young gentleman who had the honour of being nephew to the archon, and had just returned from Athens, where he had perfected himself by spending half his fortune, and transforming himself from a simple Abderite into an Athenian fop.

" The façade is pretty," modestly remarked Democritus, " and would become Athens, Corinth, or Syracuse, and, if I may be allowed to say so, I see but one fault in this splendid building."

" A fault !" repeated the archon, with an expression of countenance peculiar only to an Abderitan archon.

" A fault ! a fault ! " echoed the silly fop, laughing immoderately. " May I ask you, Democritus, what you find fault with ? "

" A trifle," replied Democritus, " only that this beautiful front cannot be seen."

" Cannot be seen ! and why not ? "

" Well, by Anubis ! how can it be seen with these ugly old houses and sheds all around, and interposing between people's eyes and the beautiful façade ? "

" Those buildings stood there long before you and I were born," answered the archon.

Dialogues of this kind often occurred, almost daily and hourly, as long as the philosopher lived among them.

" How do you like this purple, Democritus ? You have been in Tyre, have you not ? "

" Yes, madam, I have, but not that purple—
this is brought to you from Sardinia, by the
Syracusans, and sold as the purple of Tyre."

" But, at least, you will admit this veil to be
an Indian byssus of the finest kind."

" Of the best quality, lovely Atalanta, fabricated in Memphis and Pelusium."

Thus this really honest man made himself two
enemies in one minute;—could anything have
been more vexatious than such sincerity?

CHAPTER VIII.

Preliminary notice about the theatre of Abdera.— Democritus compelled to give his opinion upon it.

THE Abderites were very proud of their theatre. Their performers were common citizens of Abdera, who either could not live by their business or were too lazy to acquire one. They had no scientific notion of the dramatic art, but had consequently so much the higher opinion of their own abilities, and really they were not destitute of some talent, as the Abderites were by nature buffoons, jugglers, and pantomimists, and every part of their bodily frame assisted in giving significance to the subjects of which they were speaking. They possessed one dramatic author of their own, called Hyperbolus, who, in their opinion, had brought their stage to such a state of perfection as to be but little behind that of Athens itself. He was great in comic as in tragic compositions, and wrote the drollest satires,* in which he parodied his own tragedies in so ludicrous a style that (to use the Abderite expression) one could laugh at them till one's sides split. In their opinion Hyperbolus combined in his tragedies the sonorous versification and the powerful imagination of Æschylus with the eloquence and pathos of Euripides, as well as, in his comedies, the humour and sparkling wit of Aristophanes with the fine taste and elegance of Agathon. The facility with which he composed his works was his greatest boast. Every month he produced a tragedy, as well as a farce : "My best comedy," said he, "costs me no more than fourteen days, notwithstanding that its performance lasts four or five hours."

"Heaven be gracious to us ! " thought Democritus.

Now the Abderites, from all directions, insisted on his giving them his opinion of their theatre, and though unwilling to dispute with, or still less to flatter them, he was obliged to give his decision.

"How does this tragedy please you ? "

---

* Greek farces, resembling the Italian *opera buffa*, of which we may form an idea from the " Cyclops" of Euripides, the only piece of this kind now extant.

"It is well chosen; what kind of an author must he be who could spoil such a subject?"

"Did you not find it very exciting?"

"A piece may be very exciting in some parts, though a miserable affair as a whole," said Democritus. "I know a sculptor from Sicyon who has a passion for chiselling only figures of Venus,—they look generally like very ordinary young girls, who have the finest legs in the world. The secret of which is, that the man takes his wife for a model, who, happily for his Venuses, possesses at least beautiful legs. So the most miserable poet may succeed in a stirring part, if it happens that he is in love, or has lost a friend, or has met with any accident to make him uneasy in heart and mind, so as to be placed in the position of the person whom he wishes to depict."

"Then you do not find the 'Hecuba' of our author perfect?"

"I think that the man perhaps has done all he possibly could, but all the feathers which he plucks from Æschylus, Sophocles, and Euripides, in order to cover his own nakedness, though perhaps they do him honour in the eyes of those spectators who have not so good a recollection of all those authors as myself, only prejudice me

against him. A crow as she is created by
nature, is, in my opinion, prettier than if she
were adorned with the feathers of the peacock
or the pheasant. Generally I require from the
author of a tragedy a good production to obtain
my applause, by the same right as I expect from
my shoemaker a good pair of boots for my
money; and although I confess it is more difficult to make a good tragedy than a good pair of
boots, I am nevertheless entitled to expect from
every tragedy as many good qualities as from a
boot, *e. g.* all that belongs to a good article."

"And what do you require from a well-booted
tragedy?" asked a young Abderite nobleman,
laughing heartily at the fair conceit which he
thought he had uttered.

Democritus was conversing with a little circle
of persons, who appeared to listen to him without noticing the witty question of the young
gentleman. "The true rules of a work of art,"
said he, "cannot be arbitrary. I require no more
from a tragedy than Sophocles required from his
own, and that is, neither more nor less than what
the subject of itself will in good hands produce.
A simple, well-reflected plan, in which the author
has foreseen and prepared everything, and brought
it in a natural way to the point ; where every part

forms a necessary link, and the whole is a well-organized, free, noble, and beautiful production ; no tiresome exhibitions, no episodes, no scenes for filling up gaps, no speeches whose end is impatiently awaited, no action which does not tend to the principal object. I expect characters taken from life, noble, but not too much so for human nature ; no superhuman virtues, no monsters of wickedness; personages speaking according to their individual conceptions and feelings, so as to fill up their peculiar parts according to their past and present circumstances and destinations, as they would naturally, in case of any given event, speak and act, or they must cease to be what they are. I require that the author should be not only well acquainted with human nature as the model of his copies, but that he should have some regard for the spectators, and that he should have a perfect knowledge of the way in which he can best touch their hearts; that he should prepare imperceptibly every stroke which he intends to make, that he should know when he has gone far enough, and that before tiring us with uniform impressions, or exciting our feelings to a degree that begins to be painful, he grant us time to reflect and rest from emotion ; and that he should know how to multiply the emotions which he imparts to us, without injury to the principal action. I demand from him easy, beautiful, and polished language; expressions always powerful and warm, simple yet sublime, never too pompous or too low, but strong and nervous without being stiff or harsh, shining but not dazzling; true heroic language, which is always the expression of an elevated mind inspired by the subject immediately before it, never saying too much or too little, but fitting, as a garment adjusts itself to the body, to the conviction of the speaker. I require from one who makes heroes speak, the possession of a great soul, and that, being inspired by the power of imagination, he puts into the mouth of his hero all that he feels in his own heart. I demand——"

"O Mr. Democritus!" exclaimed the Abderites, who could not stand it any longer, " you are making many demands. You may require all you please, but in Abdera we are satisfied with much less—we are pleased if an author moves us. A man who can make us laugh or cry at pleasure, is, in our eyes, divine, and let him manage it as he likes; that is his business, and not ours. We like Hyperbolus—he moves our hearts, and makes fun for us; granting

sometimes that he makes us yawn, he is nevertheless a great author.   Do we require any
further proof?"

"The blacks on the Gold Coast," said Democritus, "dance with transport to the noise of
a pair of sheepshanks, and pieces of tin, which
they strike one against the other.   Give them a
set of cowbells and a pipe, and they will fancy
themselves in heaven.   How much wit had your
nurse, when you, as children, were moved by
her stories!—the most stupid tale sung in a
plaintive tone was sufficient.   But is that any
reason that the music of the blacks and the
tale of the nurse should be excellent in themselves?"

"You are very polite, Democritus."

"I beg your pardon.   I am so unpolite as to
call everything by its name, and so obstinate
that I will never confess that all is beautiful
and excellent which is so called."

"But the opinion of a whole people would, I
hope, be of more value than the self-conceit of a
single individual."

"Self-conceit!—that is just what I wish to see
exiled out of the realm of the fine arts.   There
is not one of all the requirements from which
the Abderites so kindly release their favourite

Hyperbolus, which is not founded upon the strictest justice; the opinion of a whole people, if it be not a sound one, may and must be wrong in innumerable cases."

"Now, by Jupiter!" cried an Abderite, who appeared to be very well satisfied with his own opinion, "you would finally argue us out of our five senses."

"Heaven forbid!" replied Democritus; "if you would be modest enough not to pretend to more than the five senses, it would be the greatest injustice to trouble you in the quiet enjoyment of them. The five senses, if all used, and properly used, are pretty good judges in all cases wherein is to be determined what is white or black, smooth or rough, soft or hard, thick or thin, bitter or sweet; a man who never goes further than he is led by his five senses, goes always on sure ground. And, in fact, if Hyperbolus takes care in his comedies that every sense is pleased while none are offended, I could guarantee them a good reception, even were they ten times worse than they are."

If Democritus had gone no further at Abdera than Diogenes did at Corinth, his liberty of speech might have brought him into serious trouble; for though the Abderites were willing enough to ridicule solemn things, they could not bear any jest upon their puppets and hobby-horses. But Democritus belonged to one of the first families in Abdera, and, which was of more importance, he was rich. For those two reasons they forgave in him what would not have been tolerated from a philosopher in a frieze cloak. " You are an insupportable man, Democritus," snarled the beautiful Abderites; but withal they bore with him.

That same evening the poet Hyperbolus composed a terrible satire on the philosopher. Next morning it was found on all the drawing-room tables in the city, and the night after it was sung in all the streets of Abdera, for Democritus had set it to music.

CHAPTER IX.

Good-humour of the Abderites, and how they succeeded in avenging themselves upon Democritus for his want of politeness.—An example.—The Abderites make a law against all travelling, in order that an Abderitan child should not become wiser than his parents.— Curious case, in which the nomophylax Gryllus decides a difficult question arising from this law.

It is commonly a dangerous thing for a man to have more sense than his neighbours. Socrates paid for his superiority with his life, and if Aristotle saved his skin, accused as he was of heresy by the chief priest Eurymedon, it was because he took to his heels in time. " I will take care," said he, "not to give the Athenians a second opportunity of sinning against philosophy." * The Abderites, with all their human infirmities, were not ill-natured—Socrates, amongst them, might have attained the age of Nestor. They would have considered him a

* Ælian, *Var. Hist.* iii. 36.

marvellous fool, and laughed at his uncommon absurdity, but to go as far as the cup of hemlock was not in their character. Democritus went to work so sharply with them that certainly a less genial people would have lost their patience. Yet all the revenge they took upon him was in speaking (without troubling themselves on what grounds) as hardly of him as he did of them. They criticized everything he undertook, treated as ridiculous all that he said, and when he ventured to advise anything, they did just the contrary. "We must bring down this philosopher," said they; "he must not fancy that he knows everything better than we do." And following out this maxim, the good people of Abdera committed one folly after another, and thought they should succeed admirably if they could but annoy him. Happily they did not attain their purpose, because Democritus only laughed at their efforts, and, in spite of all their provocation, he had not one grey hair the earlier. "Oh! the Abderites! the Abderites!" exclaimed he often; "there, they have given themselves another slap on the face, hoping thereby to exasperate me."

"But," said the Abderite ladies, "can there be a worse man? In everything he differs from us, and he always finds harm in everything that pleases us: it is very unpleasant to be always contradicted."

"But if you are always wrong," answered Democritus—and indeed how could it be otherwise?—"you are indebted for all your notions to your nurses, and your ideas are all just what they were in childhood. Your bodies are grown up, but your minds are yet in the cradle. How many among you have taken the trouble to examine upon what grounds they find a thing right, fair, or good? Like children, you fancy everything pretty and good which tickles the senses and pleases you, and on what petty causes and circumstances (often irrelative to the case) does it depend whether you are pleased or not! How embarrassed you would often be if you were asked why you were pleased with one thing and disliked another! Caprice, temper, wilfulness, the habit of being imposed upon by other people, of seeing with their eyes, of hearing with their ears, and of whistling after them the tune they have whistled—these are the motives which influence you instead of your own judgment. Shall I tell you the reason of it? You have formed to yourselves a false idea of liberty. We are, you say, a free people,

and you think that common sense has nothing
to do with you. Why should we not be allowed
to think as we please, love and hate, esteem
or despise, as we please? Who has a right to
contradict us, or to question our tastes and
feelings? So then, my dear ladies, think and
act, love and hate, wonder and despise, just
when, what, and why you please. Commit as
many follies as you like, make yourselves as
ridiculous as you choose. To whom is the thing
of any earthly consequence, so long as it is
only a matter of trifles—puppets and hobby-
horses? Who would desire to disturb you in the
exercise of your rights to pull the one and ride
the other exactly according to your own good
pleasure? Let it be granted that the doll is an
ugly one, and that what you call a hobby-horse
looks more like an ox or a donkey. What does
that matter? If your follies make you happy,
and nobody else unhappy, how can it concern
other people that they are follies? Why should
not the high council of Abdera go in a solemn
procession of leap-frog to the temple of Latona,
if it so pleased the sovereign people? But, my
dear fellow-countrymen, your absurdities are not
all so innocent as these would be; and when I
see that through your whims and fancies you

do yourselves grievous wrong, I should be no
friend of yours if I looked on and said nothing.
For instance, your pigmy war, like that of
Homer's frogs and mice, with the people of
Lemnos,—the most unreasonable and unservice-
able that ever a state engaged in : and for the
silliest cause in the world—about a ballet-girl !
It is clear that you must have been under the
unmitigated influence of your evil genius when
you resolved on it. And nothing was of any
effect that could be laid before you as against it.
The Lemnians were to be chastised, and as you
are a people of warm imagination, nothing
seemed easier to you than to take possession of
the whole island. In fact, you never see a
difficulty till you have actually run your nose
against it. Yet even all this might pass if you
had at least committed the execution of your
determination to a fit man. But to make the
young Aphron your commander-in-chief, without
any other ground than that the ladies thought
him in his new armour as handsome as Paris
himself, and to forget, in the pleasure of seeing
a great bush of flame-coloured plumes rolling
over his beardless face, that it was not a mere
review the conduct of which you were intrust-
ing to him,—this, don't deny it, was a very

E 2

Abderitish trick indeed; and now that you have paid for your folly with the loss of your honour, your gallies, and your best troops, what does it avail you that the Athenians, whom even in their follies you have taken for your masters, have been guilty of as senseless a proceeding, and have reaped just as pleasant a result?"*

In this tone did Democritus talk to the Abderites as often as they gave him the opportunity, but as these opportunities occurred very often, it can hardly be expected that they should find the philosopher's orations very pleasant ones. This is the consequence, they said, of allowing conceited young wiseacres to travel all round the world: they learn to despise their fatherland, and, after ten or twenty years, back they come as cosmopolites, with their heads full of outlandish notions, fancying that they know everything better than their grandfathers, and that

* The Athenians, in their war with Megara, had, if we may believe Aristophanes, no better reason than that some silly young nobleman of the latter city had attempted to revenge the abduction of a courtesan of their town, by carrying off a nymph of similar status from the conservatory of Aspasia. Aspasia's influence was all-powerful with Pericles, that of Pericles with the Athenians, and so came to be kindled a war with Megara. —See also Plutarch's Life of Pericles.

whatever they have seen abroad is better than what they find at home. The ancient Egyptians, who never allowed anybody to travel till he had seen at least fifty years, were wise people.

On the spot went the Abderite senate to work, and made a law that no son of Abdera should travel further than the Corinthian isthmus for a longer period than one year, or at all except under the care of a tutor well advanced in years, and of genuine Abderite stock, education, and way of thinking. Young people must indeed, declared the decree, see the world, but on that very account they ought not to stay in any place longer than is necessary for them to see what is to be seen there. The tutors shall take special notes of the hotels, the cookery, and the charges, that really useful information may be gathered for the benefit of those who may come after them.

Besides this, the law provided that the tutor should prevent the young Abderite from being entangled in any unnecessary acquaintance. The landlord of the hotel, or one of the waiters, would be able to say what was most worthy of observation in the town and neighbourhood, who were the most remarkable scholars and artists, where they dwelt, and at what time they could

be seen, all which the tutor would set down in
his note-book ; and thus in two or three days a
man who knew how to make good use of his
time, could get through a great deal of business.*

Unluckily for this wise law, it happened that
two young Abderite gentlemen of considerable
importance were out of the country at the time
when it passed, and was, according to old custom, proclaimed before the people in their usual
place of assembly.   One of these was the son
of a scrivener, who, through sharp practice and
underhanded dealings, had, in the space of forty
years, accumulated no inconsiderable fortune,
and had married his daughter, the ugliest and
stupidest animal in all Abdera, to the nephew of
the fat little alderman of whom already honourable mention has been made.   The other was
the son of the nomophylax, and it was his duty,
in order to be as soon as possible, and the sooner
the better, associated with his father in his
office, to travel to Athens, and there to study
classical music, as diligently at least as the heir
of the scrivener was making himself acquainted

* Those who imagine that this passage is an ana-
chronism will do well to consult the works of those who
have written " *de re cauponariâ veterum.*"

with the milliners and other damsels of the Attic capital.

The framers of the law had not considered the peculiar position in which these gentlemen found themselves, and the question was, what could be done?—should the law itself be modified, or should a dispensation be granted by the senate for this particular case?

"Neither one nor the other," said the nomophylax, who had just finished composing a new dance for the feast of Latona, and was exceedingly satisfied with himself. "To change anything in the laws the people must be called for, and that would only give our malcontents an opportunity for inflammatory declamation. With regard to the dispensation, it is true that the laws are mostly made for the sake of granting dispensations from their authority, and I doubt not that the senate will grant us what every one in similar cases is entitled to demand. Yet every licence looks like a favour, and I see not why we should incur any obligation. The law is a sleeping lion as long as he is not aroused, and we can walk round him as safely as round a lamb; but who would have the impudence and audacity to call forth its powers against the son of the nomophylax?"

This defender of the law was, as we may perceive, a man who had a very refined idea both of the law itself and of his position, and was always ready to make use of the prerogatives of his situation.   His name deserves to be known : it was Gryllus, the son of Cyniscus.

CHAPTER X.

Democritus goes to reside in the country, and is assiduously visited by the Abderites.—Different curiosities, and a conversation about the Schlaraffen country.

DEMOCRITUS, on his return to his own country, had flattered himself with the hope of being useful to it through the improvement of his own mind and heart. He never imagined that the Abderite heads could be in so hopeless a state; but after having resided among them for a long time, he saw clearly that the attempt to improve them would be indeed a vain enterprise. Everything among them was so disarranged that it was difficult to decide where to commence the amelioration. Every abuse hung on twenty others, and it was impossible to abolish one without transforming the whole. A good epidemic which should extirpate the whole race from the

E 3

face of the earth, save a few dozen children, would
be the only means, thought he, of helping the
state : as to helping the people, that was out of
the question.   He determined, as far as possible,
peaceably to withdraw from the company of his
fellow-citizens, and to apply to the improvement
and embellishment of his estate all that time
which he could spare from his daily study.   But
unluckily this estate lay very close to Abdera;
and as the situation was undeniably beautiful,
and the way to it one of the pleasantest walks
out of the city, it so happened that every holiday
brought about him a multitude of ladies and
gentlemen, many of them claiming relationship
with the philosopher, and making a fine day
and an agreeable walk the excuse for breaking
in upon his beloved solitude.

Now, though Democritus pleased the Abderites
as little as they pleased him, yet the effect in the
two cases was widely different.   He fled from
them because they occupied his time and wearied
him ; they followed him because he occupied
theirs, and thereby saved them from *ennui*.
He well knew what to do with his time ; they
had nothing at all to do with theirs.

" We have come to help you to pass away the
time in your hermitage " said the Abderites.

"I find my time pass quite quickly enough in my own society," was the reply.

"But how is it possible for any man to like so much solitude?" exclaimed the lovely Pytheca. "I should die of *ennui* if I were a whole day without seeing anybody."

"You do not express yourself rightly—you mean if you were a whole day without being seen by anybody."

"But who can imagine that Democritus is ever at a loss what to do with himself? Why, his whole house is filled with the curiosities which he has collected in his travels. Pardon the liberty which I take, Democritus, and let us see the pretty things you have brought home with you."

Now began the sorrows of the poor hermit. He really possessed a pretty collection of objects from the divers regions of nature,—stuffed animals, birds, fishes, and butterflies, fossils, ores, &c. Everything was new to the Abderites, everything excited their astonishment. The good naturalist was stunned with so many questions in a minute, that to answer them at once he must have been composed, like the goddess Fame, only of tongues and ears."

"Explain to us, if you please, what this is."

"What is it called?" "Where did it come from?" "How did it happen?" "Why is it so?"

Democritus explained as well as he could; nevertheless, it became but little clearer to the Abderites, or rather, they seemed to comprehend less after his explanation than before ;—it was not his fault !

" Wonderful!—incomprehensible!—very wondrous !" were their perpetual exclamations.

" It is as natural as anything in the world can be," replied Democritus, coolly.

" You are so modest, Democritus ! but probably you wish us to pay you more compliments upon your good taste and extended travels ?"

" Do not make me more your debtor, gentlemen ; I accept all your good intentions as received."

" But, at least, it must be a very pleasant thing to travel so far over the world," said an Abderite.

" And I think just the contrary," said another. " Take all the dangers and inconveniences to which one is exposed—the bad roads, wretched inns, sand banks, shipwrecks, wild beasts, crocodiles, sharks, rhinoceruses, unicorns, and winged lions, all things which swarm in Barbary."

" And, after all, what is the use of it ? " interrupted an Abderite matador ; " after having seen how vast the world is, I should think that the portion I possess of it would appear too inconsiderable to afford me any satisfaction."

" But do you count for nothing the having seen so many different nations ? " said the first speaker.

" And what is to be seen there ? People ! They can be seen at home ; every place is the same to us."

" Ah ! there is a bird without legs !" exclaimed a young lady.

" Without legs ? "

" And the entire bird with only one wing ! "

" That is miraculous," cried another ; " only fancy ! "

" And how does it fly with only one wing ? "

" Oh ! above all things, I should like to see a living sphinx," said one of the cousins ; " you certainly must have found many of them in Egypt."

" But is it possible that the wives and daughters of the Gymnosophists in India, as it is related—you understand, I hope, what it is I am asking ?—— "

" Not I, Mistress Salabanda."

"Oh, you certainly do! You have been in India —you have seen the wives of the Gymnosophists?"

"Oh yes! and you may believe me that the wives of the Gymnosophists are neither more nor less women than the wives of the Abderites."

"You do us much honour; but that is not what I wished to know. I inquired if it was true that they"—and here she put herself in the attitude of the Venus de Medici, to make the philosopher understand what she was desirous of knowing. "Well, now do you comprehend me?"

"Yes, madam, Nature has not been more niggardly to them than she is to others—what a strange question!"

"You will not understand me, Democritus. I thought I had told you clearly enough that I wished to learn if it were true that they are —must I speak plainly?—that they walk about as destitute of clothing as they came into the world?"

"Destitute!" cried all the Abderitan ladies at the same time; "why, they must be more impudent than the girls are in Sparta! But who could ever believe it?"

"You are right," said the naturalist; "the women of the Gymnosophists are less exposed than the women of Greece in their completest

dress—they are covered from head to foot
with their innocence and the public respect."*

" What is it you mean ? "

" Oh yes, I understand you—it is a joke which
is intended; but you only joke concerning their
innocence and respectability. If the wives of
the Gymnosophists are not more closely covered,
they must be very ugly, or their husbands must
be very indifferent."

" Neither one nor the other; their wives
are extremely well formed, and their children
healthy and lively,—an irrefragable testimony
in favour of their husbands, as it appears to
me."

" You dearly love paradoxes, Democritus,"
said the matador; " but you will never persuade
me that the morality of a people would be the
more pure the more exposed the women were."

" Were I as great an admirer of paradoxes
as I am suspected of being, it might perhaps
be very easy to prove to you that same by
examples and reasons ; but I do not sufficiently
admire the practices of the Gymnosophists to act
as their defender, nor was it my intention to say

* " The public respect served them for a veil," said
an old author, whose name I do not know, speaking of
the Spartan maidens.

what the wily Cratylus asserts I have stated.
The women of the Gymnosophists are only a
proof that habit and circumstances, in affairs
of this kind, decide everything. The Spartan
maidens because they wear slight dresses, and
the women of India because they wear none,
are by no means less respectable, or exposed
to greater danger, than those who enfold their
virtue in seven veils. It is not the dress,
but imagination concerning it, which awakens
the passions. The Gymnosophists consider
their wives, although clad as they are by nature alone, to be quite as well dressed as the
Scythians, whose wives have a tiger-cat's skin
wrapped around their loins."

"I should not like to see Democritus, with
his philosophy, possess sufficient influence over
our wives to put such ideas into their heads,"
said a respectable, stiff Abderite, who dealt in
furs.

"Nor I!" said a linen-draper.

"Nor I, indeed, notwithstanding that I deal
neither in furs nor linen," replied Democritus.

"But allow me to ask you one thing more,"
whispered the cousin, the same who wished to
see a living sphinx. "You have been across the
world, and there must be many places wherein

everything is different to what it is here, and it must be wondrous!"

"I do not believe one word about it," muttered the alderman, shaking the ambrosial curls on his wisdom-bearing head, like the Homerian Jove.

"Tell me, please, which of all these countries delighted you most?"

"How could any one be pleased anywhere except in Abdera?"

"Oh, we know that you are not in earnest—tell the young lady, without compliment, what you think," said the alderman.

"You will laugh at me," replied the philosopher; "but if you wish it, pretty Clovarion, I will tell you the truth. Have you never heard of a country where nature is so kind as to take upon itself, in addition to its own achievements, the work of men;—of a country where reigns an eternal peace; where there are no servants, no masters, no poor, and no rich; where a thirst for gold impels no one to crime, because gold is useless; where the sickle and the sword are alike unknown; where the industrious work not for the idle; where there are no doctors, because there is no sickness; no judges, because there are no disputes, for every one is content,

because he possesses all he desires ;—in a word,
a country where men are as gentle as lambs,
and as happy as gods ? Have you ever heard
of such a country ? "

"No, not that I can remember."

"I call that something like a country, Clovarion ! There it is never too warm, never too
cold—never too wet nor too dry ; spring and
autumn reign there, not alternately, but, as in
the gardens of Alcinous, at the same time, in
eternal concord; mountains and valleys, forests
and groves, are filled with everything which the
heart of man can desire. Not that the inhabitants take the trouble of hunting the hares,
catching the fish or the birds, or gathering the
fruit, nor have they any other trouble to obtain
the comforts they enjoy. The partridges and
snipes come around you, larded and roasted,
and humbly ask to be eaten ; the fish swim
ready boiled in ponds of sauce of every description, and the shores are covered with
oysters, lobsters, patties, hams, and smoked
tongues ; hares and roebucks voluntarily present themselves with their skins over their ears,
put themselves on the spits, and, when ready,
place themselves on the dishes. Everywhere
tables rise, the cloth is ready laid, and soft

quilted couches invite you to recline on them;
near to them gush little brooks of milk and
honey, wine, lemonade, and other agreeable
beverages; and over them, mingled with roses
and jasmine, rise arches provided with tumblers
and glasses, which, when emptied, replenish
themselves. There also are trees which instead
of fruit bear little tarts, sausage-rolls, almond-
cakes, and other dainties, over which are suspended violins, harps, guitars, lutes, flutes, and
clarions, which play of themselves, and form the
most agreeable concerts that can be imagined.
The happy people, after having slept through
the sultry hours of the day, and spent the
evening in dancing, singing, and lively conversation, are refreshed in marble baths, where
they are rubbed with invisible hands, dried by a
fire self-made and self-sustained, and perfumed
with costly essences which descend in vapour
from the evening clouds. Then they place the
softest cushions around their covered tables, and
eat, drink, laugh, sing, jest, and kiss; the
night, by means of an eternal full moon, is
merely a softer day; and what is the most
pleasing thing is——"

"Do not talk nonsense, Democritus; you are
deceiving me. All you relate is the tale about

the land of Cocaigne, which I have heard from my nurse a thousand times, when I was a little girl ! "*

" But you may imagine, Clovarion, that the living in this country must be very good."

" Do you not perceive that under all this a secret meaning is concealed ?" said the sapient alderman, " probably a satire on certain philo-

---

* [Beranger has reproduced the mediæval ideas about the land of Cocaigne in his celebrated song :—

> " Ah ! vers une rive
> Où sans peine on vive,
> Voyageons gaiement."

And Moore, in his " Fudge Family in Paris :"—

> " After dreaming some hours of the land of Cocaigne,
> That Elysium of all that is *friand* and nice,
> Where for hail they have *bon-bons,* and claret for rain,
> And the skaters in winter show off on cream ice,
> Where the fowls fly about with the true pheasant taint,
> And the geese are all born with a liver complaint !"

Some of the most pleasing of the romances and *fabliaux* of the middle ages are those which relate the discovery—alas ! for a short time only—of this realm of delight.

The Germans call it Schlaraffen land.—TRANSLATOR.]

sophers who place the supreme happiness in luxury."

"Badly guessed, worthy alderman!" thought Democritus.

"I remember having read a similar description of the golden age, in the 'Amphictyons' of Teleclides," said Mistress Salabanda.*

"The country which I have described to the pretty Clovarion is not a satire," said the naturalist; "it is the country in which twelve out of every dozen of you wise men wish to be, and all men by all means would, if possible, arrive at,— a country which your Abderite moralists wish to recommend, if their declamations have any meaning at all."

"I wish I could see how to understand this," said the alderman, who, according to his long-standing habit of hearing with half his ears,

---

* Salabanda is right. A long time before the "Manuel" of Madame Dannog, Lucian had made mention of the land of Cocaigne in his true history; and before him the Greek comic authors Metagenes, Pherecrates, Teleclides, Crates, and Cratinus, had given their descriptions of it, and the way of living therein, in which they endeavoured, by the most extravagant fancies, to leave nothing for modern writers to add. The boldest particulars enumerated by Democritus are taken from the fragments left us by Athenæus in the sixth book of his "Deipnosophists."

and giving his vote in the council asleep, never took the trouble to think long about anything.

"You are fond of a strong illustration, as I perceive, Mr. Alderman," replied Democritus; "now too much light for seeing is as bad as too little. I understand 'a clear light' to mean exactly as much light as will enable us to see clearly. This presupposes the faculty of seeing, for without this, even by the light of ten thousand suns, we could perceive no better than by that of the glow-worm."

"You are speaking of glow-worms," said the alderman, as he roused himself at 'the word from the mental sleep into which he had been thrown by gazing on the beauties of Salabanda; "I thought we had been talking about the moralists."

"Of moralists or glow-worms, just as you like," replied Democritus. "To make it more clear, the country about which we have been discoursing is one where an eternal peace exists, and where the people are in the same degree both free and happy, where the good is not mixed with evil, where sorrow borders not upon pleasure, nor virtue upon vice, only beauty, order, and harmony are found; in a word, a country such as you moralists would wish to see extend over the whole earth—a country where people have no stomach or digestion, or else such a country as that described by Teleclides, from whose 'Amphictyons,' as the fair Salabanda judiciously discerned, I have taken my description. Perfect equality, perfect contentment, and everlasting concord; in short, the Saturnian age, in which kings were not required, nor priests, nor soldiers, nor moralists, any more than tailors, cooks, physicians, or executioners, which is possible only where roasted partridges fly into the mouth, or (which means the same thing) where are no wants. This, I think, is so clear, that to any one who finds it obscure, all the light of a summer day would not render it clearer; nevertheless, you moralists are vexed that the world is as it is, and if an honest philosopher who knows why it cannot be otherwise, laughs at the anger of these gentlemen, they look upon him as the enemy of God and men, which of itself is still more laughable, but which, where those splenetic gentlemen are masters, has sometimes a very melancholy termination."

"But what must the moralist do?"

" Understand nature a little better before he attempts to improve it,—try to be more easily conciliated, and more patient with the follies and tempers of men ; to make them better by example, instead of fatiguing them with cold harangues, or exasperating them by libels ; to expect no effect where there is no sufficient cause ; and not to aspire to reach the top of the mountain without the trouble of ascending it."

" No one would be so foolish," said one of the Abderites.

" So foolish are nine out of ten of the legislators, project-mongers, schoolmasters, and reformers of the world, all over the globe, and in every age," said Democritus.

The company, who had been only in search of amusement, now began to find the humour of the naturalist intolerable, and went home, but dallied long on the way, beguiled by the splendour of the stars and a beautiful twilight into endless reveries amongst sphinxes, unicorns, Gymnosophists, and the country of Cocaigne ; and notwithstanding the variety of stupidities which had been spoken, all agreed that Democritus was a wonderful, conceited, overwise, censorious, yet very amusing and original person. " His wine is the best thing that appertains to him," said the alderman.

"Gracious Anubis!" thought Democritus when left alone, "what strange things one must say to these Abderites to beguile the time with them!"

CHAPTER XI.

A little talk about the philosophers of Abdera, and how
Democritus had the misfortune to get into discredit
through some well-intended observations.

It must not be imagined that the Abderites,
without exception, were bound by a vow, or by
their oath of citizenship, not to possess more
understanding than their grandmothers, nurses,
or aldermen. Abdera, the rival of Athens,
possessed also philosophers—that is, she had
philosophers just as she had painters and poets.

The celebrated Protagoras was an Abderite,
and left a great many disciples, who, if they
equalled not their master in wit and eloquence,
surpassed him at least in sophistry and self-
conceit.

These gentlemen had arranged an easy sort of
philosophy, by which they could find without
difficulty an answer to every question, and speak
so fluently of all that was under or over the
earth, that, as they had always Abderites for

hearers, their auditors gave them credit for knowing more than themselves, notwithstanding that the difference between them was not sufficient for a wise man to give a fig for. Certainly it was a fact, that the Abderite philosopher, except a few long and unmeaning words, knew no more about the matter than the rest. The philosophers, because they thought it unworthy of their greatness to descend to the details of nature, dealt only with propositions lying beyond the borders of the human understanding; to these regions, thought they, nobody will follow us but persons of the same calibre with ourselves, and we are sure not to be found liars, whatever we choose to tell the Abderites.

For instance, one of their favourite subjects was the question, " Why, wherefore, and wherefrom, was the world originated ? "

" It began from an egg," said one of them ; " the air was the white, chaos was the yolk, and water bred it." *

* To avoid erroneous conjectures being formed by those readers who have not read Diogenes Laertius, or Deslandes, or Brucker's " Critical History of Philosophy," or the compendiums of Messrs. Formeyd and Birsching, the author reminds them that all these hypotheses can boast very respectable antiquity, and have had many critics

" It originated in water and fire," said another.

" It never began," said a third ; " all was ever as it is, and will remain so to eternity."

This last opinion was applauded in Abdera, it being the easiest solution of the question.

" It explains everything," said they, " without compelling a man to wear out his brains."

" All was ever as it now is," was the common reply of an Abderite when he was asked the reason or origin of anything ; and he who was not satisfied with the answer was declared to be a blockhead.

" What you call the world,"said a fourth, " is probably a succession of worlds, which, like the skins of an onion, lie one upon another, and detach themselves one after another."

" Very clearly explained," cried the Adberites, " very clearly." They thought they understood the philosopher, because they knew what an onion was.

" Nonsense ! " said the fifth. " There are of course innumerable worlds, but they originate from the accidental movements of indivisible solar atoms, and it is a comfort if, after ten

and adherents. The opinion of our Democritus is the only one which (probably because it was the most sensible) has not produced a sect.

thousand failures, one comes forth looking so sweetly sensible as ours."

" I concede the atoms," said the sixth, "but there are no movements by accident and without direction. The atoms are nothing, or they have certain forms and qualities, and, accordingly as they resemble each other or not, they attract or repel each other. For this reason the wise Empedocles, the man who, in order to learn the true construction of Ætna, threw himself into its crater, recognized love and hate as the first motives of every composition, and Empedocles is right."

" I beg your pardon, gentlemen, you are all wrong," said the philosopher Sisamis ; " never will a world arise from all your eggs, nor from the union of water and fire, nor from your atoms, nor from your homœomerias, if you call not the spirit to your aid. The world, like every animal, is a composition of spirit and matter. The spirit is that which gives form to the sub- stance, and both are united, but as single bodies are dissolved as soon as the spirit, which keeps all the parts together, has with- drawn, so, in the same manner, if the general world-spirit should cease to embrace and ani- mate all, heaven and earth would dissolve at the same moment into a dark, formless, and inert mass."

"Jupiter and Latona preserve us!" cried the Abderites, not without alarm on hearing the wise man utter such a frightful threat.

"No danger," said the priest Strobylus; "as long as we have the frogs of Latona within our walls, the world-spirit of Sisamis will not have the trouble of bringing about so much disorder."

"Friends," said an eighth, "the world spirit of Sisamis is of the same value as the homœomeria, onions, atoms, and eggs, of my comrades; we must have a world-maker (a demiurgus) in order to have a world, because a building requires a builder, or at least an architect, and nothing can arise from nothing, as we all know."

"But is it not an every-day expression, a thing happens of its own accord or it arises spontaneously?" said the Abderites.

"It is usual to say so," replied the philosopher, "but have you ever found that it so happened in reality? I have indeed heard Archontes say a thousand times, 'it will happen,' 'the result will be,' 'this or that will necessarily arise'; but we had to wait long enough for it—it neither happened, came, nor spontaneously arose."

"Very true as concerns the work of your

Archontes," rejoined an old bootmaker, who was esteemed by the people an intelligent man, and had great expectation of being shortly elected master of the cordwainers' guild; "but with the work of nature as the world is, it must be another affair. Why should not the world have sprung from chaos, as the mushroom springs from the earth?"

"Master Awl," replied the philosopher, "to be the head of your corporation you shall have my vote, and those of all my relatives, but you must not object to my system if you please! The mushroom grows by itself from the earth, because it is a mushroom, but a world cannot be grown from itself, because it is not a mushroom; do you understand me now, Master Awl?"

All present laughed heartily at the discomfiture of Master Awl. "The world is not a mushroom, that is as clear as daylight," cried the Abderites; "you cannot confute this, Master Awl."

"Confound it!" murmured the future chief of the corporation, "but it is always so if one associates with gentlemen who can prove so logically that snow is white."

"You mean to say it is black, neighbour?"

"I know what I said and what I meant," replied Master Awl, "and I only wish that the republic——"

"Do not forget the fourteen votes which I can procure you, Master Awl," cried the philosopher.

"Well, well,—very well! But the demiurgus, it sounds half like demagogue, and I will have neither demagogues nor demiurgus; I am for freedom, and whoever is a good Abderite will toss up his hat and follow me."

And with these words Master Awl went away, (the reader must remember that all this passed in a hall of Abdera,) and several idle fellows, who used always to accompany him, followed him out.

But the philosopher, as if he had not observed it, continued :—"Without a builder, or a demiurgus, or whatever name you give it, the world could not have been built; but please to remark, it depends upon the superior whether he is willing to build or not, and let us see how he would probably proceed. Imagine, then, matter as an immense mass of perfectly formed crystal,* and the creator shattering with a great diamond hammer this mass, at one

* This philosopher was, it seems, a Cartesian before Descartes.

blow, into a vast multitude of infinitely small pieces; imagine that through empty space they were broken into *some* particular forms, and that they occupied, at intervals, many millions of square miles. Of course these infinitely diverse particles of broken crystal, thus put in motion by the violent stroke of the diamond hammer, and flying in a thousand directions, clashing, beating, and rubbing each other, produced an innumerable number of those little bodies of every kind of figure, regular and irregular, triangular, quadrangular, octangular, multiform, and circular. From the spherical came water and air, which is nothing more than thinner water, from the triangular fire, from the others earth; and these four elements are the natural components of all other bodies in the world."

"This is wondrous, very wondrous! but it can be conceived," said the Abderites; "a mass of crystal, a diamond hammer, and a creator who breaks in so masterly a way this crystal in pieces, that from the splinters is produced, without further trouble, a world! This is indeed the most acute hypothesis that can be conceived, and moreover so simple that any one might have found it out for himself in a moment."

" I explain, by this simple presupposition, all possible operations of nature," said the philosopher with a self-satisfied smile.

" No, not even a wasp's nest," called out a ninth, named Demonax, who had been hitherto listening to the assertions of his fellow-citizens with silent contempt. " There must necessarily have been a wise design and preparation to bring about so vast, so beautiful, so wonderful a thing as this system of the universe. A perfect wisdom could alone have devised the plan, though I confess that for the execution inferior workmen might have been employed. The great creator portioned out this labour to the different classes of subaltern gods, assigning to each class its own circle in which it might work, and was content for himself to assume a general inspection over all. It is ridiculous to attempt to explain the origin of the universe, the earth, the planets, the animals, and all that is in the air and in the water, by atoms, sympathies, accidental motion, or a single stroke of a hammer. There are spirits who reign in the elements, who turn the spheres of the heavens, who form organic bodies, who embroider the spring-robe of nature with flowers, and pour the fruits of autumn into her bosom. Can there exist anything at once more reasonable and more pleasing than this theory? It explains everything, refers every effect to a suitable cause, and by it we understand what by every other system is inexplicable, namely, the art of nature, just as easily as men understand how Zeuxis and Parrhasius can create with a little coloured earth their splendid landscapes, or those still more splendid scenes from our mythology."

"What a pretty thing is philosophy!" said the Abderites; "the only fault to be found with it is the difficulty of making a choice among so many theories."

In the mean time the Pythagorean, who had attributed all to these informing spirits, was the most successful. All the poets, painters, and other cultivators of the Muses, headed by the ladies of Abdera, declared for the spirits, but with the proviso of being allowed the liberty of arraying them in the form that was most pleasing to each.

"I never was a special friend of philosophy," said the priest Strobylus, "and for good reasons. But if the Abderites cannot leave off inquiring about the how and the why of everything, I have less to object to the physics of Demonax

than to any other; with due limitations they at
least may be tolerated."

"Oh! it agrees with everything in the
world," said Demonax; "that is the beauty
of it."

"Shall I tell you my opinion?" said Democritus. "I think, if you are really anxious to
learn the properties of things around you, you
take a hugely circuitous way of doing it. The
universe is very great, and from the point of
view from which we see it, it is so far to its
principal provinces and metropolitan cities, that
I cannot imagine how any one of us can fancy
himself capable of mapping out a country of
which (his native town excepted) all that remains, even to the extent of its limits, is unknown. I think that before we dream about
cosmogonics and cosmologies, we should do
well to contemplate the origin of something
within our reach—say, for example, a spider's
web; and this as long as it may be necessary
to find out all that the five senses, aided by the
intellect, can discover about it. You will find
work enough, take my word for it; this spider's
web will disclose more to you concerning the
system of nature, and give you more worthy
notions about its creator, than all these fine world

systems that you have excogitated in your brains between sleeping and waking."

Democritus was quite serious, but the Abderite philosophers thought he was making a mockery of them. "He does not understand anything about pneumatology," said one. "Of physics much less," said another. "He is a sceptic, he believes in no original impulse, in no world-spirits, in no demiurgus, not even in a God!" said the first, second, third, fourth, fifth, sixth, and seventh philosophers. "Such people are not to be tolerated in the republic," said the priest Strobylus.

CHAPTER XII.

Democritus retires further from Abdera.—How he employs himself in his solitude.—He is suspected by the Abderites of practising magical arts, which gives him an opportunity of making an experiment on the Abderite ladies, and how it ended.

NOTWITHSTANDING all this, Democritus was a philanthropist in the real sense of the word, for he was well intentioned towards mankind, and was never better pleased than when he could prevent evil or do good, either by practising it himself or furthering it in others. And although he believed that the character of a cosmopolite bore proportions to which, in case of collision, all others must yield, he yet felt himself not the less bound as a citizen of Abdera to interest himself in the state of his country and to assist in its improvement as much as possible. But as only so much could be achieved as the sub-

ject was capable of admitting, he found, by the
innumerable impediments raised against him by
the Abderites, his ability reduced within such
narrow limits that he had reason to look on himself as the most superfluous person in the republic.
" What they most want," thought he, "and the
best thing I could do for them, would be to
make them wise; but the Abderites are a free
people, and if they won't be wise, who can compel them?"

Consequently, since, through the before-named
circumstances, he was unable to do anything for
the Abderites, as Abderites, he thought himself
justified in placing his own person in safety
as much as possible, and in securing as much
time as he could to devote to his cosmopolitan
duties.

For that purpose his present residence was
not far enough from Abdera, for, from its agreeable situation and other conveniences, it presented
too many attractions to the Abderites, so that, notwithstanding his remaining in the country, he was
always surrounded by them; he removed, therefore, some miles further into a forest belonging to
his property, and built in the wildest part of it a
small house where he devoted himself to retire-
ment (the only proper element of the philosopher

and the poet), giving most of his time to the
investigation of nature and scientific contempla-
tion.

Some modern learned men—whether Abderites or not, we will here leave undecided—have
advanced many opinions as to the occupations of
this Greek Bacon in his solitude,—very natural
ones, though wonderful enough. " He tried to
find out the philosopher's stone," said Borrichius, " and he found it, and produced gold," in
proof of which he appeals to a book written by
Democritus about stones and metals.

The Abderites, his fellow-citizens and contem-
poraries, went further still, and their conjectures
(which, in Abderite heads, soon turned into cer-
tainties) were established on grounds as good as
those of Borrichius. Democritus had been
educated by Persian Magi,* and he had been
travelling for twenty years in the East, had
associated with Egyptian priests, Chaldeans,
Brahmins, and Gymnosophists, and was initiated
in all their mysteries, had brought with him a

* Xerxes, who, in his march against the Greeks, had
his head-quarters for some time in the house of the father
of Democritus in Abdera, was much attached to the
young Democritus, and left a couple of magicians whom
he had with him to assist in his education.—*Diog. Laert.*

thousand secrets from his travels, and knew ten thousand things of which never before an Abderite had entertained any idea. Did not all these put together afford undeniable proof that he was a perfect master in the art magic? Why, worthy Father Delrio would have burned all Spain, Portugal, and the Algarves, upon half the evidence.

But the good Abderites possessed still more satisfactory proofs that their countryman was a little given to witchcraft. He predicted eclipses of the sun and of the moon, famine, epidemics, diseases, and future events. He had prophesied, from her hand, to a light-headed girl that she would be a Lais, and to an alderman of Abdera whose whole life was spent in eating and drinking, that he would die of indigestion; and both events had really occurred. Besides, books with unknown characters had been seen in his study; he had been found occupied in many probably magical operations with the blood of birds and animals; he was seen making decoctions from suspicious plants, and some young men affirmed to having seen him by a pale moonlight amongst graves. "To frighten him we disguised ourselves under hideous masks," said they, "horns, cloven feet, long tails; nothing was omitted. We blew

smoke from our noses and ears, and made so
stunning a noise around him that Hercules himself would have fainted through fear. But
Democritus heeded us not, and when it seemed
to him to have lasted too long, he only said, ' How
long is this childish play to continue?' "

" It is evident," said the Abderites, " that all
is not right with him; spirits are nothing new to
him,—he must know well how he stands with
them! He is a magician."

" Nothing can be more evident," said the
priest Strobylus; " we must look a little closer
after him."

It must be stated that Democritus, either
through inadvertence, or (what is far more
probable) because he did not care very much
about the opinion of his countrymen, had given
occasion for many of these evil rumours ; in fact,
it was impossible to live long among the Abderites without being tempted to make fun of them.
Their curiosity and credulity on one hand, and
the high opinion they entertained of their own
sagacity on the other, provoked everybody ; and
besides this there was no other way of being
indemnified for the annoyance of their company.
Democritus was not seldom in this case ; and, as
the Abderites were stupid enough to take in a

literal sense all he told them ironically, all the fables and absurd opinions in the world were placed to his credit, and many ages after his death were received as facts by other Abderites, or at least, unjustly enough, related on his authority.

Democritus dealt too, amongst other sciences, with that of physiognomy; and, partly from his own observations, partly from those communicated to him by others, had formed for himself a theory of it which he thought (very wisely, we believe) was to be treated in just the same way as the theory of poetry, or of any other art. For as nobody can become a good poet or painter by the knowledge of rules alone, but only those who, by native genius, long study, determined application, and continued practice, have learned how to apply them, so the art of judging by the physiognomy, of a man's interior qualities, can be useful only to those who possess great experience, observation, and discernment; to all others it can but be uncertain and deceptive, and for that reason must ever be reserved for the small number of Epoptes,* or adepts in

* Epoptes: those so called were persons who, after having passed an examination, had been admitted to a view of the great mysteries of Eleusis.—See Warburton's Divine Legation, vol. i. p. 155 of the 4th edition.

the "secret sciences and great mysteries of philosophy."

This way of thinking would have proved to any reasonable people that Democritus was not a charlatan, but to the Abderites it proved only that he was making a secret of his knowledge, and they never ceased, as often as they had any opportunity, to tease him to reveal it to them. The Abderitan ladies were especially tormented by their curiosity; they wanted to know by what external marks a faithful lover could be recognized, if Milo of Crotona* had a very large nose, if paleness was a certain sign of being in love, and hundreds of similar questions, with which they so much fatigued his patience that finally, to get rid of them, he bethought himself of frightening them a little.

"You never would have imagined, I am

---

* A man of whose wonderful strength and voracity the Greeks related the most astonishing things: for instance, that he carried on his shoulders for three hundred paces an enormous fat ox, and, after killing it with a single blow of his fist, devoured it in one day. He it was who rent an oak in sunder, but was caught in the rebound. Those who wish to know how, may consult Lough's magnificent statue, a cast of which is in the Crystal Palace.

sure," said Democritus, "that virtue could have an infallible mark in the eyes."

"In the eyes!" exclaimed the Abderite ladies; "oh, that is impossible. Why in the eyes?"

"It is a fact," replied Democritus, "and, if you will believe me, this mark has often discovered to me more secrets of young and old beauties than they would have been disposed to trust me with." *

The confidence with which he said this produced some changes of colour, notwithstanding that the Abderite ladies, in all cases which concerned the common security of their sex, used faithfully to stand by each other, and they insisted that his presumed secret was a chimera.

"You compel me by your disbelief to tell you more," continued the philosopher. "Nature is full of such secrets, my fair ladies, and why should I have wandered from Ethiopia to India if my trouble had not been rewarded? The Gymnosophists, whose wives, as you know, walk about quite undressed, taught me many things."

"Give us an instance," said the fair Abde-

---

* This is called by Chrysostom Magnenus, in his life of Democritus, a sagacity hated by the half of mankind.

rites, " among others, a secret which if I were a married man I had rather not know."

" Ah ! now we know the reason why Democritus will not marry," cried the pretty Thrysallis.

" Just as if we did not know long before," said Salabanda, " that his Ethiopian Venus made him indifferent to us Greek ladies ! Now then, the secret, Democritus, if it may be told to modest ears."

" As a proof that it can be, I will reveal it to all the beauties here present," answered the naturalist ; " I know an infallible method of making a lady tell in her sleep, with a distinct voice, all that she has in her heart."

" Get along with you ! " cried the Abderite ladies ; " you think to alarm us, but we are not so easily frightened."

" Who ever thought of frightening you," said Democritus, " by merely showing you the means by which every respectable lady may have an opportunity of proving to her husband that she has no secrets which he should not know ? "

" Would your method also operate on the unmarried ? " asked an Abderite lady who seemed neither young enough nor handsome enough to have much interest in such a question.

"It operates from the tenth to the eightieth year," replied Democritus, "without regard to any circumstances in which a woman may be placed."

The affair began to look serious. "But you are jesting, Democritus," said the wife of a legislator, not without some secret fear of the contrary.

"Will you try it, Lysistrata?"

"Try it! why not?—on condition that no magic shall be brought into use, as, by the aid of your talisman and spirits, you could make a poor woman say what you like."

"Spirits and talismans have nothing to do with it; everything is done by natural means and the most simple in the world."

The ladies, in spite of all the airs of courage which they forced themselves to assume, began to show some uneasiness, much to the amusement of the philosopher. "If we were not well aware that you are a joker, and sport with the whole world—but may we ask in what the method consists?"

"As I told you, the most natural in the world; a very little harmless thing placed at the bosom of a sleeping lady, this is the whole secret, but it performs wonders, you may believe me : it makes them speak from the innermost corner of the heart, as long as anything is to be discovered."

Of the seven ladies who were in the company, only one remained unchanged in gesture or behaviour. You will perhaps say she was old, or ugly, or miraculously virtuous, but you would be wrong in all this : she was only —deaf.

" If you wish to be believed by us, Democritus, name the means."

" I will whisper it in the ear of the husband of the lovely Thrysallis," said the malicious naturalist.

The husband of the lovely Thrysallis was, without being blind, as happy as a blind man with a pretty wife is esteemed to be by Hagerdorn ; he had always good company at his house, or at least such as was called so in Abdera. The good man thought that everybody was well pleased with his society, and with the verses which he used to read them. In fact, he had the talent of reading pretty well his miserable poetry, and because he paid attention only to his reading, he did not discern that his

hearers, instead of listening to him, were co-
quetting with the pretty Thrysallis.

In short, the senator Smilax was a man
who had too good an opinion of himself to
suspect the virtue of his wife.

"It is nothing more," whispered the philosopher, "than the tongue of a living frog,
which is to be placed on the left breast of a
sleeping lady; but in drawing out the tongue
you must take care not to withdraw any part
attached to it, and the frog must be cast again
into the water."

"The means may be good," said Smilax in a
low tone, "but it is a pity that it should seem
rather questionable. What would the priest
Strobylus say to it?"

"Never mind that," replied Democritus; "a
frog is not a Diana; the priest Strobylus may
think as he pleases, and, besides, the frog would
not lose its life."

"May I tell anybody else?" said Smilax.

"Of course, every man in the company may
know it, and every one may without fear discover
it to all the gentlemen of his acquaintance; only
with this condition, that he does not reveal it to
his wife or his betrothed."

The worthy Abderite ladies did not know

what to think of this matter; it appeared to
them not impossible—and what _would_ appear
impossible to the Abderites? Their husbands
and lovers were not very much easier, and each
secretly resolved to try the means pointed out
without delay, and all, the happy Smilax excepted, expected to learn more than they wished.

"I dare say," said Thrysallis to her husband,
with a friendly tap on his cheek, "you know me
well enough not to need such a trial; is it not
so, my dear?"

"I should like to see my husband entertain
such an idea," said Lagisca; "a trial supposes a
doubt, and a man who doubts the virtue of his
wife——"

"Is in danger of seeing his doubts changed
into a certainty," added Democritus, seeing that
she hesitated. "Is that what you mean, fair
Lagisca?"

"You are the enemy of women," exclaimed
the Abderite ladies all together; "but, Democritus, do not forget that we are in Thrace, and
be warned by the fate of Orpheus."

Although uttered in joke, there was some
earnest in this. Of course it is not quite the
thing to occasion any one a sleepless night, a
design from which we cannot declare our philo-

sopher free, as he might easily foresee the consequences of his conceit; in fact, it occasioned
so much anxiety to the seven ladies, that they
did not close their eyes the night following;
and as the supposed secret of Democritus went
the round of Abdera the next day, it produced
a total sleeplessness on the part of its female
population for several succeeding nights.

Meanwhile the ladies repaired in the day the
loss of their rest by night; and as many among
them forgot that the *arcanum* could be as well
applied by day as by night, and the ladies forgot to fasten their sleeping-room doors, the husbands gained an unexpected opportunity of
making use of the frog's tongue.

Lysistrata, Thrysallis, and several others, who
had the most to dread, were the first upon
whom the experiment was tried, with the result
which might easily be foreseen. But this soon
re-established peace in Abdera. The husbands
of those ladies, after having repeated the experiment two or three times without success,
came running to our philosopher to inquire the
cause of the failure.

"Really!" said he to them, "has the frog's
tongue had no effect?—have your wives made
no confession?"

"Not a word, not a syllable!" said the Abderites.

"So much the better!" cried Democritus; "it is a triumph for you. If a sleeping lady, with a frog's tongue applied to her breast, says nothing, it is a proof that she has nothing to say. I must congratulate you, gentlemen; every one among you may be proud of having such a Phœnix of a wife in his house."

Who could be more happy than these Abderites? They returned home as quickly as they came, and, falling on the necks of their astonished wives, suffocated them with kisses and embraces, and voluntarily confessed what they had done to be the more convinced of that virtue which (they added) they had never for a moment held in doubt.

The good women scarcely knew whether they were to believe their senses. But, though Abderites, they had the presence of mind soon to recover themselves, and bitterly to reproach their husbands for such an instance of mistrust as that of which they accused themselves. Some went so far as even to shed tears, but all had much difficulty to conceal the joy produced by this unexpected confirmation of their virtue; and though, for the sake of consistency, they were obliged to abuse Democritus, there was not one who would not have embraced him for the good service he had rendered them. To be sure, this was not what he had intended, but the result of the joke taught him a lesson, that it was not advisable, without great caution, to trifle with the Abderites.

Thus, as all things in this world have more than one side, so it happened that from the mischievous trick which our philosopher had played off on the Abderites, proceeded a great deal more good than would have taken place had the frog's tongue operated. Husbands made their wives happy by their perfect confidence, and wives their husbands by their unwonted complaisance. Nowhere in the world were seen happier marriages than in Abdera, and, for all this, the foreheads of the gentlemen were as smooth, and the ears and tongues of the ladies as chaste, as they were—in other places.

CHAPTER XIII.

Democritus proposes to teach the Abderite ladies the language of birds, which gives rise to a curious illustration of how they educated their daughters.

IT happened on another occasion, that on a beautiful spring evening Democritus was present at a party at one of those country villas with which the neighbourhood of Abdera was embellished.

"Really, embellished?" Surely, not exactly so, for when had the Abderites learned to comprehend that nature is lovelier than art, and that between making a thing artificial and embellishing it there is a great difference? But we will not discuss this further at present.

The company were reclining in a circle on a soft turf, intermixed with flowers, beneath a lofty arbour. A nightingale was singing in the branches of a neighbouring tree. A young girl about fourteen years old seemed to feel some delight in that melody which the others neither understood nor cared for. Democritus took notice of this. The girl had a sweet countenance, and much gentle intelligence in her eyes. " Pity that you are an Abderite!" thought Democritus; "of what use is your sensitive mind in Abdera?—it can only make you unhappy. But there is little danger. All that the educational care of your mother and grandmother may have left unspoiled, will be ruined by the foppish sons of our archons and aldermen; and what these spare, your female friends will entirely destroy. Four years hence you will be an Abderite young lady like the rest, and will learn that a frog's tongue placed on the breast means nothing.

" What are you thinking of, pretty Nannion?" said Democritus to the girl.

" I think I should like to sit under those trees, and listen undisturbed to the nightingale."

" Silly thing!" said her mother; " did you never hear a nightingale before?"

" Nannion is right," said the fair Thrysallis; "for myself, I could listen to nightingales all my life. They sing with such spirit, and there is something so voluptuous in their modulations, that I have often wished I could understand what they say. I am sure we should hear the prettiest things imaginable. But you, Demo-critus, who know everything, do you understand the language of the nightingale?"

"Why not?" replied the philosopher, with his usual phlegm; "and the language of other birds too."

"Really?"

"You know that I speak always in earnest."

"Oh! that is delightful. Quick! translate us something from the language of that nightin-gale. What was that which he sang just now, and by which little Nannion was so excited?"

"It cannot be translated into Greek so easily as you imagine, fair Thrysallis; we have no ex-pressions in our language which would be suf-ficiently tender and passionate."

"But how can you understand the language of birds, if you cannot repeat to us in Greek what you have heard?"

"The birds do not speak Greek, and yet they understand each other."

"You are not a bird, but a sly man, who is always laughing at us."

"What a sad fashion it is in Abdera to think ill of one's neighbours! Your question, how-ever, deserves a clearer explanation. The birds do understand each other by a certain sympathy, which, under ordinary circumstances, can only exist among creatures of the same kind. Every tone of a singing nightingale is the living expression of a sentiment, and in the listener the unison of the same feeling. He understands, by means of his own inward feelings, what the other wishes to express, and just in the same way I understand it too."

"But how do you manage to do so?" asked several of the ladies.

This question, after Democritus had so clearly expressed himself, was too Abderitish to remain without an appropriate reply. He deliberated for a moment.

"I understand Democritus," said the little Nannion, humbly.

" *You* understand him, you conceited thing!" snarled her mother. " Well, let us hear, puppet, what it is you understand about it."

" I cannot put it into words, but I feel it," replied Nannion.

" You see she is quite a child," said the mother, " though she has grown up so quickly that many persons have taken her for my younger sister. But let us not be interrupted by the babbling of a silly girl, who does not understand what she is talking about."

"Nannion has feelings," said Democritus; "she finds the key to the universal language of nature in her heart, and perhaps she understands more of it than——"

"Well, sir, do not make the foolish little girl more conceited, if you please. She is quite impertinent and snappish enough, without your encouragement."

"Bravo!" thought Democritus; "if this continued, there might be hope for the head and heart of the little Nannion."

"Let there be an end of this," exclaimed the lady, who, without knowing how and why, had the undeserved honour of being the mother of a girl characterized by feeling and intelligence. "You were explaining to us how it happened that you understand the language of birds."

It is our duty not to conceal that all Democritus had said about his knowledge of the language of birds was regarded by the Abderites as mere imposture; but this was no reason why the continuance of the conversation should be less interesting, because nothing could gratify them more than listening to things they did not exactly believe, and yet wished to believe, such as sphinxes, sirens, sibyls, goblins, spectres, and other things in the same category, and the language of birds did certainly, they thought, belong to it.

"It is a secret," said Democritus, "which I learned from the chief priest of Memphis, on being initiated into the Egyptian mysteries. He was a tall, slender man, had a very long name, and a still longer snow-white beard, which reached down to his girdle. He looked so solemn and mysterious, in his tall pointed cap and sweeping mantle, that you would have taken him for a being of another world."

The attention of the Abderites was visibly increasing. Nannion, who was sitting rather behind, listened with her left ear to the nightingale; but from time to time, as often as her mother looked in another direction or kissed her dog, she cast a grateful glance on the philosopher, to which he responded with an encouraging smile.

"All the secret," he continued, "is this :— Under certain constellations, cut off the heads of seven different birds, whose names I cannot reveal; let the blood flow into a little hole made for this purpose in the earth, which cover with laurel, and go your way; after the lapse of twenty-one days, return to the hole, open it, and you will find a little dragon of strange con·formation, which sprang from the decay of the fixed blood." *

"A dragon!" exclaimed the ladies, with every sign of astonishment.

"Yes, a dragon, though not larger than a

* Pliny, who, in his History of Nature and Art, has mingled together in the strangest manner truth and fable, relates in chap. 49 of his 10th book, with great seriousness, that Democritus named in his writings certain birds, whose blood when mixed produces a snake possessing this quality, *that he who eats it* (he says nothing about vinegar and oil) *will understand what the birds say to each other.* In this, and other similar absurdities, with which, as he says, the works of Democritus abound, he has garnished his text in another part of his works in the style of a schoolmaster. But Gellius (*Noct. Attic.* lib. x. cap. 12) defends with better reason our philosopher than Pliny condemns him. Democritus could not help it if the Abderites were stupid enough to take all he said in earnest for irony, and all he said in jest for earnest; or how could he, after his death, prevent Abderitan heads from mis-conceiving, and publishing, on his authority, thousands of stupidities which he never dreamed of? What lamentable stuff Magnenus, in his *Democritus Redivivus*, makes him say! And what must the people of the other world suffer from what is said concerning them in this!

common bat. You take this dragon, cut it in small pieces, and eat it with a little vinegar, oil, and pepper, without leaving a bit. You retire afterwards to your chamber, sleep twenty-one consecutive hours; and after this dress, go into your garden, or into an orchard, and you will not be a little surprised to find yourself instantly surrounded and welcomed by birds, whose language and song you understand as well as if all the days of your life you had been nothing else but a goose, a magpie, or a turkey-cock." *

Democritus uttered this with so much calm earnestness, that the Abderites could not do otherwise than believe, as, in their opinion, he could not have related the story with so many details were it not true. Yet they had learned only enough to make them impatient to learn all.

"But," asked they, "what kinds of birds are to be used? Are the sparrow, the magpie, the nightingale, the raven, the owl, &c., among

* This is certainly a mistake of the translator of Democritus, as it is well known that turkeys were unknown to Aristotle himself, and unknown they must have been, because they came to us from the West Indies. *Vide* Buffon, *Histoire Naturelle des Oiseaux*, t. 3, p. 187.

them? What is the dragon like? Has it wings—and how many? Is it yellow, green, blue, or rose colour? Does it vomit fire?—and if touched, does it bite or sting? Is it good to eat? What is its flavour? Is it digestible? What is to be drunk with it?"

All those questions with which the good naturalist was assailed, made him so warm, that he thought the best way to get rid of them was to confess that he had composed the whole story as a joke.

"Oh! you cannot make us believe that," cried the fair Abderites; "you are only unwilling that we should know your secrets. But we will not give you a moment's rest, depend on it! We will see, touch, smell, taste the dragon, and eat it with the skin or bones, or—you shall tell us why."

BOOK II.

HIPPOCRATES AMONG THE ABDERITES.

CHAPTER I.

A digression concerning the character and philosophy of Democritus, which the reader is requested not to pass over.

WE do not know how Democritus contrived to get rid of all these curious women. This example will, however, show how a mere accident might make the innocent naturalist appear Abderite enough to believe all the fables which he fastened on his countrymen. Those who reproach him with this have appealed to his writings, but long before the times of Vitruvius and Pliny a great many counterfeited books, with promising titles, were issued under his name. It is well known how common this kind of swindling was with the Greeks of the later period ; the names of Hermes, Trismegistus,

Zoroaster, Orpheus, Pythagoras, Democritus, were respectable enough to make purchasable the poorest compositions of the emptiest heads, especially after the Alexandrian school of philosophy had brought the art of magic into great repute; and this had given to their wise men a taste for showing themselves off to the vulgar as powerful magicians who had found the key to the world of spirits, and discovered all the secrets of nature. The Abderites had given Democritus the reputation of being a magician because they could not conceive how, otherwise, he could know so much more than themselves; and later impostors fabricated books of magic under his name, taking advantage of his reputation with the ignorant of their time.

Generally the Greeks were rather partial to making fools of their philosophers. The Athenians laughed heartily when listening to their witty farce-writer, Aristophanes, who told them that Socrates held the clouds to be goddesses, that he could measure how many flea-feet a flea could leap,* that when meditating he

* Nothing is more probable than that Socrates really said something to give rise to this farcical assertion. He had only to say in some society, speaking of greatness and littleness, that it was a common mistake to

ordered himself to be suspended in a basket to
prevent his thoughts from being attracted to
and absorbed by the earth, &c., &c.; and it was
very pleasant to them to hear the man who told
them true, and consequently very disagreeable
things, talking, at least on the stage, absolute
nonsense.

And how badly treated by his laughter-loving
countrymen was Diogenes, who of all the disciples of Socrates was the most like him. Even

describe things as large or small, without noticing the
standard by which we estimate them. He might have
told them, in his jesting way, that it was wrong to
measure the leap of a flea by the Attic yard; we must,
in order to make a comparison between the elasticity of a
flea and that of a ballet-dancer, not take the human
foot, but the flea foot as a measure, if we intend to do
justice to the flea; and such like. Now, if there was an
Abderite in the company, we may be sure he would
relate this as an absurdity that had escaped the philosopher, and represent it in his own manner; and though
Aristophanes was wise enough to understand that
Socrates had said a wise thing, it was enough for a man
of his profession, and answered his purpose of making
the philosopher ridiculous, if the words of Socrates
could only by a little perversion have the sense he
chose to set upon them—just such a meaning as would
satisfy the Athenians, who (except in taste and wit)
were tolerable Abderites.

the inspired Plato and the profound Aristotle were not exempt from imputations by which it was endeavoured to bring them down to the level of common men. What wonder, then, that the man who was so mistaken as to think and talk reasonably among the Abderites was not better appreciated!

Democritus laughed sometimes, just as we all laugh, and had he been living in Corinth, Smyrna, Syracuse, or elsewhere, he would not have laughed more than any other honest man who, from principle or temper, preferred laughing to crying over the foolishness of men ; but he was living amongst *Abderites.* It was the custom of these worthy people to be always doing something at which a sensible man must either laugh, cry, or be angry ; and Democritus laughed when Phocion would have frowned, Cato have railed, and Swift have stormed. By a tolerably protracted stay in Abdera the look of irony would probably become habitual, but to say with a certain poet who liked a little exaggeration, that he was always " on the broad grin,"* is more than any one would venture to do in plain historical prose.

* " Perpetuo risu pulmonem agitare solebat
    Democritus."—*Juvenal*, Sat. x. 33.

This report may be so much the more readily*
passed over inasmuch as the much esteemed
philosopher Seneca vindicates our friend Democritus on this point, and even considers him
worthy of imitation. " We must endeavour,"
says Seneca,* " to look at the follies and requirements of the multitude, not as deserving of
hate, but ridicule; and we should do well to
take as an example Democritus, rather than
Heraclitus:—the one going amongst mankind
thought proper to weep, the other to laugh; one
saw in all our conditions mere want and misery,
the other mere trifling and childishness. It is
more humane to laugh at man's nature than to
be angry with it, and he who laughs at the
world deserves better from mankind than he
who laments over it; the former leaves at least
a little hope, the latter stupidly mourns over
things which he despairs of seeing improved.
He also who casting his eyes over the universe
cannot restrain his laughter, displays a more
elevated mind than he who cannot refrain from
tears, for he shows that what appears to others
great and important enough to excite the most
violent emotion is so inconsiderable in his eyes

* *De Tranquill. Anim.* 15.

* as to call forth in him only the most trifling and indifferent."

After having said all this, Seneca declares that it would be better, and more worthy of a wise man, to bear quietly and calmly the prevailing faults and mistakes of men, than to laugh or cry at them. I think he might find out with little trouble something better even than this. Why should we laugh always or cry always? There are foolish men and things that deserve to be laughed at, there are others which are serious enough to extort a sigh from the philanthropic; others, which would put a saint out of patience; others, which must be borne with as proceeding from the weakness of humanity. A wise and good man (*nisi pituita molesta est*, says Horace wisely) laughs or smiles, pities or weeps, excuses or pardons, according to persons, things, places, or seasons; and again, laughter and tears, love and hate, punishment and pardon, all must have their appointed times, says Solomon, who was older, wiser, and better than Seneca, with all his antitheses.

By the way, I think the decision of the sophist Seneca is right, although he would perhaps have done better not to produce such far-fetched

reasons, or to place them in such artificial juxta-
position. However, as we have stated, the
very fact that Democritus was living among
the Abderites, and laughing at them, makes the
sin of which he is accused (however far it be
carried) one of the most excusable that was
ever brought against a wise man. Homer
makes his gods burst into inextinguishable
laughter about a far less laughable subject,
namely, the limping Vulcan, who, from a good-
hearted intention, and to promote peace amongst
the Olympians, performs the office of cupbearer!
But the allegation that Democritus deprived
himself voluntarily of sight, and the reason
why he did it, only prove, among those who
believe it, an inclination which does little
honour to their intellects. And what inclination
may that be? I will tell you, dear friend, and
may gracious Heaven direct that my words be
not spoken entirely to the winds!

It is an inclination to take as an unexcep-
tionable witness every blockhead, every mischievous simpleton, the moment that he lays to the
charge of a great man some exuberant nonsense
of which any common-place man possessing his
five senses would scarcely be guilty. I should
gladly believe that this inclination is not so gene-

ral as the despisers of human nature affirm ; but
this at least is taught by experience, that the
petty anecdotes which are circulated about great
men, at the expense of their understanding,
find easy credence with the generality of mankind.   Perhaps, however, this inclination may
not be more culpable than the pleasure that
astronomers derive from looking at the spots on
the sun.   Perhaps it is the strangeness and un-
expectedness that render those discoveries so
pleasant.   Besides, it happens not unfrequently
that the poor people who impute absurdity to a
distinguished man, think they are doing him, in
their way, a great honour, and this probably
was the case in many Abderite minds concerning the wilful blindness of our philosopher.

Democritus deprived himself of his sight, say
they, in order to be able to think more deeply.
What is there so incredible as this ?   Have we
not examples of wilful mutilations of a similar
kind—Combabus,—Origen ?   Well, Combabus
and Origen made a great sacrifice—a sacrifice
that not a few would have avoided by the loss of
all their eyes, even had they as many as Argus ;
but then they had a great motive in so doing.
What would not a man give to save his life ?
And what would he not do or suffer to remain

the favourite of a prince, or even to become a demigod? But Democritus could not have so strong an inducement. The thing would have been credible had he been a metaphysician or a theologian. There are people who can spare their eyes from their business—they generally work by their imagination, and this might possibly, for anything we know to the contrary, improve by physical blindness; but who ever heard of an observer of nature, a dissector, or an astronomer, putting out his eyes in order to be better able to observe, to dissect, or look after the stars?

This absurdity is so manifest that Tertullian attributes the assumed act of our philosopher to another reason, but one which he himself must have seen was just as absurd, had it not been necessary for his argument to overthrow Democritus, and for that purpose to make him into a mere man of straw. " He deprived himself," said Tertullian, " of sight because he could not look at a woman without emotions which he felt to be excessive."* A pretty motive for a philosopher of the age of Pericles! Democritus, who certainly never imagined himself to be wiser than Solon, Anaxagoras, or Socrates, found it necessary to take refuge in such a method! It is true that the

* Apology, c. 46.

advice of the last-named,* which was not unknown to Democritus, because he possessed enough intellect to come to the same conclusion himself, told very little against the power of love, and a philosopher who had consecrated his whole life to the study of the truth, was certainly bound to guard himself against so tyrannical a passion; but of this Democritus, at least in Abdera, could have entertained little fear. The Abderite ladies were indeed beautiful, but kind nature gave them stupidity as an antidote to their personal charms. An Abderite lady was only lovely before she opened her mouth, or till she was seen in a morning dress. To a reasonable man who was not an Abderite, she could only inspire a three days' passion, and a love of three days' duration would, to Democritus, be so little hindrance to his philosophizing, that we would advise all naturalists, anatomists, geometricians, and astronomers, to make frequent use of such a prescription against hypochondriasis, if it were not presumable that these gentlemen are wise enough not to require our advice. Whether Democritus tried the power of this remedy with any one or more of the Abderite beauties with whom we have become acquainted, we cannot, for want of authentic

* *Memorab. Socrat.*, lib. i. c. 3. num. 14.

information, decide; but that he, in order not to be captivated, or not to be too strongly captivated, by such harmless creatures, among whom he was certainly in no danger of having his eyes scratched out, should have been weak enough to scratch them out himself—this Tertullian may believe as long as he pleases, but we doubt whether anybody else will believe it with him.

But all these absurdities would appear trifling, if compared with those which a collector of materials for a history of the human understanding, although meritorious in its way, calls the philosophy of Democritus.* It would be difficult from a heap of ruins, stones, and broken pillars, brought together under the idea of being the ruins of the great temple of Olympia, to prove with certainty that these were really the fragments of that temple; but what would be thought of a man who should put together in all haste these fragments one upon the other, patching the whole together with lime and straw, and present this piecemeal work, without plan,

* Brucker, not to speak of Magnenus, who makes Democritus talk, alternately, sense and nonsense, just according to his own fancy.

foundation, grandeur, symmetry, or beauty, as
the temple itself?

Besides all this, it is very improbable that
Democritus ever constructed a system at all. A
man who spends his life in travels, observations,
and experiments, seldom lives long enough to
put all the results of what he has seen and
experienced into the form of a technical system,
and in this respect Democritus, even if he lived
more than a century, may certainly be said to
have been prematurely overtaken by death; but
that a man of such penetration and thirst after
truth as was unanimously attributed to him by
all writers of antiquity, should affirm palpable
nonsense, is a little more than improbable.
"Democritus," we are told, "explained the crea-
tion of the world solely from atoms, from empty
space, from necessity, from destiny,—he questioned Nature for eighty years, and she replied to
him not a word about her author, his plan, or
his design. He attributed to all atoms the same
kind of motion, and did he not perceive that
from elements moving in parallel directions for
ever no organized bodies could arise? He denied
that the cohesion among atoms existed in the
ratio of their resemblance to each other—he explained that all within the universe—the world—

existed by an infinitely quick but blind motion, and yet affirmed that the world was a whole—a complete work."

These and other absurdities are placed to his account. Stobæus, Sextus, Censorinus, are quoted, and without taking the trouble to inquire whether it is in the category of possible things that a man of intellect, for which Democritus is famed, should reason so miserably. It is true that great geniuses are no more exempt than little ones from the possibility of error, and from drawing wrong conclusions; it must be allowed that they fall far more readily into those faults than the Lilliputians would wish to believe. But there are absurdities which only a blockhead can imagine or assert, as well as crimes which can only originate with a villain. The best men have their anomalies, and the wisest of human beings may suffer sometimes a momentary eclipse; but we may, notwithstanding this, assert with tolerable security, that he will in all ordinary cases act and speak as a man of intellect may be expected to do, and that especially when and where blockheads are collected together.

This maxim, if well applied, may save us through life from many rash judgments—many mistakes in distinguishing between appearances and truth, some of which may produce weighty results. That it would help the Abderites I doubt, for there is just one thing necessary in the application of the maxim which they did not possess. The good people used to keep a stock of logic quite different from that of reasonable men, and many notions were associated in their heads which, but for the Abderites, would never, to all eternity, have existed together. Democritus examined the nature and observed the consequences of certain natural events, a little sooner than they; therefore he was called a sorcerer. His thoughts were generally the reverse of theirs, he lived on other principles, he spent his time alone, and in a manner incredible to them; hence they decided that all was not right in his head. " *The man*," said they, " *has studied too much*," and they were apprehensive that the results would turn out very unsatisfactory after all.

CHAPTER II.

Democritus is charged with a serious crime, and is defended by one of his relatives, on the ground that he was not in his right mind.—How he succeeds in allaying the storm raised against him by the priest Strobylus,—a specific which seldom fails in effect, if well applied.

"HAVE you heard anything about Democritus?" said the Abderites to one another. "For six whole weeks nobody has seen him; he cannot be found, or, if met with, he sits absorbed in thought, and you may stand before him for half an hour, speak to him, and go away, without his perceiving it. Sometimes he examines the entrails of dogs and cats; sometimes he boils herbs, or stands with a great pair of bellows before a magical furnace, and makes gold, or perhaps something worse. In the daytime he climbs like a goat the steep cliffs of Mount Hæmus, in order to search for plants, as if he had none nearer home; and by night, when even the irrational creatures seek repose, he wraps himself in a Scythian fur, and peeps—by Castor!—through a blowpipe at the stars."

"Ha! ha! ha! ha! nothing could be imagined more ridiculous. Ha! ha! ha!" laughed the thick, short alderman.

"After all, I pity this man," said the archon of Abdera; "it must be confessed that he knows a great deal."

"But what profit is it to the republic?" replied a senator who by his projects, improvements, plans, and reductions of old outs and ins, had pocketed a good round sum from the republic, and on this account trumpeted forth in all societies his extraordinary share in the preservation of Abdera—although Abdera was not a hundred drachmas the richer for all his projects, reductions, and improvements.

"That is true," said another; "he spends all his knowledge on mere playthings, nothing solid! *In minimis maximus.*"

"And his insupportable pride!"

"His spirit of contradiction!"

"His eternal reasoning, criticizing, and jesting!"

"And his bad taste!"

" Of music, at least, he understands nothing," said the nomophylax.

" And of the drama still less," interposed Hyperbolus.

" Of lyric poetry he is equally ignorant," said Physignathus.

" He is a charlatan," * said a stump-orator.

" And a free-thinker, above all," cried the priest Strobylus, " a finished free-thinker, a man who believes in nothing, and with whom nothing is sacred : it can be proved that he has extracted the tongues from living frogs."

" It is strongly rumoured that he has dissected many while yet alive," said somebody.

" Is it possible? " cried Strobylus, with marks of the deepest disgust. " Could it be proved, just Latona ! to what may this infernal philosophy bring a man ! But could it be really proved? "

" I repeat it as I heard it," replied the other.

" It must be inquired into," replied Strobylus ; " most honourable archon, gentlemen of

* The translator of this book recalls with pride the appellation " literary charlatan," applied to himself for writing books and lecturing on philosophical subjects to working men : the term was used by a clergyman who thought such proceedings out of the clerical sphere, and who certainly never wandered from his own in that direction.

the senate, I require you, in the name of Latona, to inquire into this matter."

"But why an inquiry?" cried Thrasyllus, one of the heads of the republic, a near relative and presumptive heir to the philosopher; "the fact is in some degree true, but it proves nothing more than what I have long since perceived in my poor cousin, that all is not so right with his intellect as could be wished. Democritus is not a wicked man—he is not a heretic, but there are times when he is not himself. I am certain that whenever he dissected a frog, he mistook the frog for a cat."

"So much the worse," said Strobylus.

"In fact, so much the worse for his head and his affairs," continued Thrasyllus. "The poor man is in a state to which we cannot any longer be indifferent; the family will be compelled to call upon the republic for assistance; he is by no means capable of administering his property; he must be placed in confinement."

"If this be so——" said the archon with a thoughtful mien, and stopped short.

"I shall have the honour to acquaint your excellency with fuller particulars," replied the senator Thrasyllus.

"What! Democritus insane!" exclaimed one

who was present. "My lords of Abdera, reflect well upon what you are doing; you are in danger of becoming objects of ridicule to all Greece. I will lose my ears if on this side of the Hebrus, or on the other too, you can find a clearer-headed man than Democritus. Be cautious, gentlemen; the matter is more delicate than you think."

Our readers are astonished, but we will assist them immediately out of their wonder: he who thus spoke was not an Abderite, he was a foreigner from Syracuse; and the reason that he was held in esteem by the magnates of Abdera, was, that he was a relative of the elder Dionysius, who had recently risen to be prince of that republic.

"You may be sure we shall not proceed further in the matter than we find necessary," replied the archon to the Syracusan.

"I am so much interested in the honour which the noble Syracusan by his good opinion does my cousin," said Thrasyllus, "that I should wish to be able to second it. It is true Democritus has his lucid intervals, and in one of those has perhaps had the honour of conversing with the prince; but, alas! they are only intervals."

" Then the intervals in Abdera must be very long," said the Syracusan.

" Noble and learned gentlemen," said the priest Strobylus, " the circumstances may have been as you state, but I must remind you that the discourse was about living frogs being dissected. The fact is serious, and I urge upon you an inquiry into the matter; Apollo and Latona demand it, and I should fear——"

" Calm yourself, reverend sir," interrupted the archon, who was himself suspected of a less devout way of thinking concerning Latona's frogs than could be wished for in a citizen of Abdera. " On the first motion presented to the senate by the Board of the Sacred Pools, the frogs shall have the most complete satisfaction."

The Syracusan immediately informed Democritus of all that had been said at this party.

" Put the fattest peacock* in the poultry-yard

* This seems to be an error in the text. The peacock was unknown to Greece before the conquest of Persia by Alexander, and long after it had been introduced from Asia into Europe, it was so rare that it was shown in Athens for money. In a short time, however, it became, to use the expression of the dramatic author, Antiphanes, as common as " *quails*." In the luxurious times of Rome they were brought to market in great quantities, and the peacock was an important dish on the

upon the spit," said Democritus to his house-
keeper, "and tell me when it is ready."

That same evening as Strobylus sat at his
table the roasted peacock was brought in on a
silver dish, as a present from Democritus.
When opened it was found to contain a hundred
gold darii.*

"This looks not so bad for the intellect of
the man," thought Strobylus.

The remedy operated immediately as far as
was intended. The high priest enjoyed the
peacock exceedingly, drank with it a bottle of
Greek wine, put the hundred darii in his pocket,
and thanked Latona for the satisfaction she had
procured for her frogs.

Roman table. Whence Buffon could have derived the
opinion that the Greeks never ate the peacock, I cannot
tell; he might have learned the contrary from a passage
of the poet Alexis in Athenæus. It is, however, true
that if peacocks were not known in Europe before Alexander, Democritus could not have sent one to the priest
Strobylus. It may, on the other hand, be supposed that
the naturalist had brought a peacock among other curiosities from India; and why may it not be supposed?
If necessary, we could relieve ourselves from the difficulty
by means of the coins of Samos—on which Juno is represented with a peacock—were it worth the trouble.

* A Persian coin, supposed to have been first struck
by Cyaxares II., or Darius of Media, after the conquest
of Babylon.

" We have all our failings," said Strobylus on the following day at a great party. " Democritus is, it is true, a philosopher, but I find he is not so ill-intended as his enemies say : the world is censorious, odd stories have been circulated about him, but I always like to think the best of everybody. I hope his heart is better than his head. There may be something not right in the latter, and for my part I suspect it is so. To a man under such circumstances much must be forgiven. I am sure he would be the most accomplished man in Abdera if his philosophy had not turned his brain."

Strobylus, by this speech, killed two birds with one stone: he acquitted himself of his obligations towards our philosopher, by speaking of him as a good man, and he gained the good-will of the senator Thrasyllus by throwing a doubt on the soundness of Democritus's intellect. All which shows that the priest Strobylus was, with all his simplicity, if you like to call it so,—a very sharp practitioner.

CHAPTER III.

A little digression to the government of Shah Baham.—
The wise character of the senator Thrasyllus.

THERE is a kind of men who may be known
and observed for many years without its being
determined whether they are wicked, or merely
weak. Scarcely have they committed an action
of which a man with a little reflection would be
incapable, when they astonish us with such an
elaborate piece of malice, that, with all good-will
on our parts to form the best opinion of their
hearts, we feel compelled to bring them in
guilty. We took it for granted yesterday that
Mr. Such-an-one was so weak that it would be
a sin to reckon his follies against him as crimes;
to-day evidence equally good convinces us that
he is too spiteful to be simply a blockhead—we
cannot find an excuse to free him from the guilt
of a malevolent intention; but scarcely have we

made up our minds about this when he says or does something to throw us back upon our former hypothesis, or at least to place us in that unpleasant state of mind which arises from not knowing what to think of the man, or, if our unlucky stars bring us into any kind of contact with him, how on earth we are to act.

The secret history of Agra relates that the celebrated Shah Baham found himself in a similar case with regard to one of his Omrahs. The Omrah was accused of having committed an injustice.

" Well, then, he shall be hanged," said Shah Baham.

" But, sire," said one, " the poor Kurli has so weak a mind that it is uncertain whether he even knows the difference between his right hand and his left ; he may not be aware whether he has committed an injustice or not."

" If so, send him to a lunatic asylum," said the Shah Baham.

" Nevertheless, sire, as he has sense enough to avoid a loaded wagon, and pass by a post against which he might otherwise break his head, because he perceives that the post will not go out of the way to pass by him——"

" Oh ! does he perceive that ?" inquired the

Shah Baham. "By the beard of the prophet! say not another word—to-morrow it shall be seen whether there is justice in Agra."

"Meanwhile there are people who will assure your majesty that the Omrah, excepting his stupidity, which sometimes makes him so mischievous, is the most respectable man in the world."

"I beg your pardon," interrupted one of the courtiers present, "just the contrary! All that is good in Kurli he owes to his stupidity—he would be ten times worse than he is, had he sufficient intellect to know what he is about."

"Do you not see, my friends, that in all you say there is not one word of common sense?" replied Shah Baham. "Compare your opinions together, if you please. One says Kurli is a mischievous man because he is stupid. No, says another, he is stupid because he is mischievous. Nonsense, says a third, he would be a mischievous man were he not so stupid. What can I make out of all this nonsense? Let somebody tell me what to do with him; he is too spiteful, it seems, for a lunatic asylum, and too stupid for the gallows."

"The case is this," said the Sultana Dinarzade; "Kurli is too stupid to be very mischievous, and yet he would be less mischievous if he were less stupid."

"The plague take such an enigmatical fellow!" said Shah Baham; "here are we sitting and racking our brains to find out whether he is a fool or a rogue, and, after all, you see that he is both at once. Considering all this, I have made up my mind what to do. I will leave him undisturbed; his wickedness and his stupidity will keep each other in balance. So long as he is not an Omrah, he will do no great harm either through one or the other. The world is wide; Mashallah! let him go. But, before you do so, tell him to come and thank the Sultana. Three minutes ago I would not have given a fig for his neck."

It was for a long time a difficult problem to find out why Shah Baham was surnamed "the Wise" in the annals of Hindostan, but, with this decision before us, there need be no longer any question about it. All the seven wise men of Greece could not have untied the knot better than Shah Baham.

The senator Thrasyllus had the misfortune to be one of these (happily for the world) not very ordinary men, in whose heart and head stupidity and wickedness (as the Sultan expressed himself) were neutralized by each other. His designs on the property of Democritus were not new. He had relied on his cousin, after so long an absence, never again returning, and took the trouble to form a plan upon this supposition, which, by his return, was frustrated in a very unpleasant manner. Thrasyllus, whose imagination was already accustomed to see in the inheritance of Democritus a part of his own fortune, could hardly get reconciled to considering the matter in any other light. He consequently regarded the philosopher as a robber who kept him out of his property; and, what made the matter worse, the robber had the law on his side.

Poor Thrasyllus thought over many ways of counteracting these unfavourable circumstances, and thought for a long time in vain; at last he believed he had discovered, in the behaviour of the naturalist, a ground upon which to base his injurious projects. The Abderites are already prepared, thought Thrasyllus; as it was in Abdera a decided point that Democritus was insane, it was only necessary to make a legal representation to the great council that his insanity went so far as to disable him from being his own master. This presented, however, some difficulties.

Thrasyllus, with his unaided intellect, would not have succeeded; but such worthies can always find rogues whose abilities are for sale, which is almost the same thing as having the talent themselves.

CHAPTER IV.

THERE was in Abdera a class of people who
lived upon the art of making all kind of wrong
appear right, and giving a good appearance to
bad affairs. Their chief modes of proceeding
may be reduced to two—they consisted in falsifying the facts, and in perverting the law; and
as the business was very profitable a great many
persons commenced it, and finally the bunglers
elbowed out the masters. The profession lost
by this much of its respectability. Those who
did the business were called sycophants,* because
they were mostly such poor wretches that for a

---

* Sycophants, fig-eaters; a class of persons not unknown out of Abdera,—only there they ate figs, here
they eat what they can get.

fig they would say or do anything that was required of them.

Meanwhile, as the sycophants formed at least a twentieth part of the inhabitants of Abdera, and as they could not live entirely on figs, it may be easily imagined that the ordinary occasions from which law-suits could arise were not sufficient for their maintenance. The sycophants of an earlier age waited till their assistance was asked, but their successors, had they adopted the same etiquette, would have been reduced to the sad alternative of starving or working. Begging was not allowed in Abdera (which, by the way, was the only thing that foreigners found praiseworthy in the police of the city).

Now the sycophants were too lazy to dig, and, in consequence, nothing remained for them but to make for themselves the requisite employment. The Abderites were very passionate in their tempers, and had but little discretion, so that opportunities of profiting thereby were not wanting. Every opportunity produced a lawsuit. Every Abderite had his own sycophant, and thus a kind of equilibrium was established, through which the profession grew to be held in greater consideration, inasmuch as competition sometimes elicited great talent.

Abdera by this means won the glory of falsifying facts and perverting laws to a greater degree than even Athens itself; and this repute became in time profitable enough to the State. For then every one who had a disreputable suit of any consequence to conduct wrote for a sycophant from Abdera; and it was a very natural consequence that such sycophant never left his client until he had gained from him all that was to be gained.

But this was not the only profit which the Abderites obtained from their sycophants,— what in their estimation was the most to be prized in those persons was the comfort of being able to practise every sort of roguery without having the personal trouble of it, or coming into direct contact with the law. After having intrusted a sycophant with an affair, a man might generally be easy about the result. I say *generally*, because, in fact, there had been cases in which the sycophant, after having been well paid by his employer, had, notwithstanding, helped the adverse party in his claim. But this had only occurred when the adversary paid him at least three times more than he obtained from his legitimate client.

As for the rest, nothing could be more admir-

able than the good understanding existing in
Abdera between the sycophants and the magistrates. The only persons to whom this concord
was not advantageous, were the clients: in all
other enterprises, however dangerous and bold
they might be, there was a possibility of coming
out scatheless; but an Abderite client was always sure to lose his money, whether he or his
suit lost or won. Well, the people quarrelled
neither more nor less on that account, but their
notions of *justice* obtained so bad a repute,
as only Abderites could be indifferent to,
that it became a proverb in Greece to wish
an enemy nothing worse than a law-suit in
Abdera.

But, through this digression about the sycophants, we had nearly forgotten that our imme-
diate subject was the project of the senator
Thrasyllus for obtaining the fortune of our philosopher, and the means by which he intended
to commit this robbery under the protection of
the law.

In order not to tire our readers with too many
details, suffice it to say that Thrasyllus intrusted
the case to a sycophant: he was one of the cle-
verest in Abdera,—a man who despised the common tricks of his professional fellows, and piqued

himself on being able to say that since he had carried on his honest business he had won some hundreds of the most deplorable cases without uttering a single direct lie. He leaned always upon undeniable facts, but his strength lay in combination and in "*chiaro oscuro.*" Democritus could not have fallen into better hands. We only regret that, as the proceedings of the whole law-suit have long ago mouldered away, we are unable to present to young and aspiring sycophants the entire speech by which this great master of the art proved to the court of Abdera that Democritus ought to be set aside from the management of his own affairs. All that remains of this speech is a small fragment, which appears to us sufficiently characteristic to show how these gentlemen could twist facts at their pleasure ; and as it will occupy but a few pages of this history, we shall lay it before the reader.

"The greatest, the most dangerous, the most insupportable of all fools," said he, " are reasoning fools; without being the less foolish, they conceal from the unreflecting crowd the disorder of their heads by the dexterity of their tongues, and are reputed wise because they rave more coherently than their fellows in the asylum. An unlearned fool is lost if he happens to speak nonsense. But with the learned fool it is just the contrary,—his fortune is made, and his fame established, as soon as he begins to speak or to write absurdity; for the greater part of mankind, though aware that they understand nothing of what is thus said or written, either are too suspicious of their own intellect to perceive that the fault does not lie in themselves, or too stupid to remark, and too vain to confess, that they are so entirely in the dark on the subject.

"The more nonsense the learned fool talks, the louder the unlearned fools cry 'Wonderful!'—the more busily they puzzle their heads to find sense in high-sounding absurdity; and as a dancer jumps the higher the louder he is applauded, so these clap the more in order to see the learned buffoon perform greater wonders; and so it happens that the levity of one spirit takes possession of the multitude, and that, as long as the fashion for nonsense exists, altars are erected to the very man who, under other circumstances, would be just placed without ceremony in a lunatic asylum. Fortunately for our good town of Abdera, we have not gone so far. We acknowledge and confess, with one voice, that Democritus is an original, a fantastic character; but we are satisfied with only laughing at him—and it is in that we are wrong: now, we laugh at him, but ere long we shall perceive something extraordinary in his folly. From astonishment to admiration is only a step, and when we have commenced this, Gods! who can tell where we are to stop? Democritus is a humourist, we say now, and we laugh; but what kind of a humourist is Democritus? A conceited free-thinker, a scoffer at our old customs and regulations, an idler, whose trifling occupations are of no use whatever to the State, no more than if he did nothing at all,—a man who dissects cats, who understands the language of birds, and seeks after the philosopher's stone,—a necromancer, a butterfly-hunter, a star-gazer! And now can we any longer doubt that he ought to be placed in confinement?

"What would become of Abdera if his folly grew contagious? Shall we prefer awaiting the consequences of such an evil, instead of embracing the only means by which we can prevent it? Happily for us, the laws afford us this method. It is simple, it is certain, it is right. A dark cell, most wise fathers,—a dark cell! Thus we shall be at once out of danger, and Democritus may rave as he likes.

" ' But,' say his friends (for, fool as we all admit him to be,.we have so far gone in the course to which I have adverted, that he possesses partisans among us), 'where are the proofs that his insanity has reached such a point that we are bound in law to have recourse to the dark cell?' Truly, if, after all we know, we ask for more proofs, I suppose he must take red-hot coals for gold pieces, or look for the sun at noonday with a lantern, before we shall be convinced. Has he not asserted that the goddess of love was black in Ethiopia? Has he not endeavoured to persuade our wives to walk about naked, as do the wives of the Gymnosophists? . Has he not recently affirmed in a large assembly, that the sun is stationary; that the earth turns round her axis 365 times in the year; and that the reason we do not fall into empty space is owing to a magnet placed in the centre of the earth, attracting us like so much file-dust, though we are not made of iron? But I will concede that all these are trifling things; one may speak foolishly and act wisely. Would to Latona that the philosopher were in a similar case! But, I am sorry to be obliged to say it, his actions prove so great an amount of insanity, that all the hellebore in the world would not be sufficient to clear the brain in which it has been produced. In order not to abuse the patience of the high senate, I will only cite two out of numberless instances, which can be legally proved, should there be a doubt of their probability.

" Some time ago, some figs were brought to our philosopher, which, as it seemed to him, had a strange taste of honey. It appeared to him to be a very serious thing. He left the table, walked to the garden, ordered the tree from which the figs had been gathered to be shown to him, and, after examining the tree from top to bottom, ordered it to be dug around at the root, searched into the earth in which it grew, and I doubt not also into the constellation under which it was planted. In fact, he puzzled his brains for several days in calculating how and in what form the atoms must connect themselves with each other, to give the taste of honey to a fig. He found out one hypothesis, then rejected it, and adopted another, then a third, a fourth, and dismissed them all because not one appeared to him sufficiently subtle and learned. It interested him so much that he lost his appetite and his sleep. At last his cook took pity on him. ' Sir,' said she, ' if you

had not been so learned, you would have discovered why the figs smelt so of honey.'

" ' And why ?' asked Democritus.

" ' I placed them, to keep them fresh, in a pot
in which honey had been before,' said the cook ;
' this is all the secret, and I think there is
nothing more to examine into.'

" ' A pretty explanation you are giving me,'
said our world-wise philosopher ; ' it may satisfy
such a simple creature as yourself, but do you
think it satisfies me?   Or, even granting such
was the case, as you say, what does it import to
me?   Your honey-pot certainly shall not stop
my investigations as to how such a thing might
happen without any honey-pot at all ; ' and so the
wise man continued, spite of his own reason and
of the cook's, to search deeper after the truth
than into the honey-pot, in which, nevertheless,
it had been concealed, until some other fancy,
coming in contact with this, led him into other,
and probably still more absurd researches.

" But ridiculous as this anecdote may be, it
is nothing in comparison with the proof of
sense which he gave last year when the olives
in Thrace and all the contiguous districts failed.
Democritus had the year before prophesied, I
do not know whether by geomancy or other

magic art, that olives, which were then very
cheap, would be an entire failure in the following year. Such knowledge would be enough
to make the fortune of a sensible man for the
rest of his life. It really appeared, at first, as if
Democritus was not willing to lose this opportunity, as he bought up all the oil in the
country. A year after, the price of oil rose—
partly because the crop failed, partly because
the stores were in the hands of Democritus—
to four times the value of its cost. Now I put
it to all men who know that four is four times
more than one, to guess what this man did?
Can you conceive that he was insane enough to
give the oil to the persons of whom he purchased it, at the price he had paid for it ?*   We

* How differently this fact may be related! While
it seemed to the sycophant as the complete proof of an
insane mind, Pliny speaks of it as a noble action—doing
honour to philosophy. Democritus was too good-hearted
to become rich at the cost of others who could not
afford it so well as himself. Their anxious trouble and
despair at having lost so great a profit, moved him. He
gave the oil, or the money he received for it, and was
satisfied to show the Abderites that it only depended on
himself to acquire riches if he thought it worth the
trouble. In this light Pliny sees it; and, in fact, it is
necessary to be an Abderite, a sycophant, or a rogue, to
speak of it in the manner of our advocate.

know, too, how far the generosity of a man who is in possession of his senses may be stretched; but this action lies so far beyond the bounds of credibility, that even the people who gained by it shake their heads and are doubtful as to the sanity of a man who looked upon a heap of gold as a heap of nutshells. Unfortunately for his heirs, they appear to be only too much in the right."

CHAPTER V.

It is resolved that the case shall be decided by medical opinion.—The senate sends a letter to Hippocrates.—The physician comes to Abdera.—Appears before the court.—Is invited by the senator Thrasyllus to a banquet, and half killed with *ennui.*—An instance that a purse full of daries has not a good effect on every one.

So far goes the fragment, and, judging of the whole by so small a part, the sycophant really deserved more from the senator than a basket of figs; it was not his fault, certainly, that the senate of Abdera did not commit our philosopher to a dark cell. But Thrasyllus had antagonists in the senate, and Master Awl, who in the mean time had become head of his corporation, affirmed very strongly that it would be acting against the freedom of Abdera to declare a man insane before he was acknowledged as such by an impartial physician.

"Well," said Thrasyllus, "so far as I am

concerned, you may inquire of Hippocrates himself; I shall be satisfied."

Did we not say a little while ago that the wickedness of the senator Thrasyllus was balanced by his stupidity? It was a silly trick to call in Hippocrates in such a dubious case, but he did not expect to be taken at his word.

" Hippocrates," said the archon, " is the best man to get us out of this difficulty. Fortunately, he is just now staying in Thasos; perhaps he may be induced to come over to us, if we ask him in the name of the republic."

Thrasyllus changed colour a little on finding that they received his proposal seriously, but the majority voted with the archon. A deputation was sent at once, with an invitation * to the doctor, and the senate spent the remainder of the sitting in deliberating upon the honours with which he should be received.

This was not such an Abderite resolution,†

* There is something about this in an edition of the works of Hippocrates; but it is, without doubt, an interpolation, and is the work of some sly Græculus of latter times, as well as the relation of the interview of that physician with Democritus, in one of the forged letters which bear the name of the former.

† At least, so the physicians may think who are found amongst our readers.

but where have we said that the Abderites never could do anything like wiser people? Meanwhile, the reason that they paid such great honour to Hippocrates was not on account of the esteem they felt for him, but only from the vanity of being recognized as a nation who know how to value a great man. And besides, have we not remarked, on another occasion, that they were always very fond of festivities?

The deputation was ordered to say nothing more to Hippocrates than that the senate of Abdera required his presence and decision in a very important case; and Hippocrates, with all his philosophy, could not imagine what sort of important business it could be. Why should they make a secret of it?" thought he; "surely the corporation of Abdera has not been attacked by a disease which nobody is willing to divulge!"

Meanwhile he determined with the greater willingness to undertake the journey, as he had long wished to make acquaintance with our philosopher; but great was his surprise when, after being met with great pomp, and conducted before the whole assembled senate, he was informed by the reigning archon, in a most elaborate speech, that he was called over to Abdera only for the purpose of examining as to the sanity of their fellow-countryman Democritus, and to give his opinion whether there were any means of curing him, or, if he were too far gone, to declare him, without hesitation, to be civilly defunct.

" It must be some other Democritus," thought the doctor at first, but the gentlemen of Abdera left him not long in doubt. " Well, well," said he to himself, " am I not in Abdera?—how could I forget it?"

Hippocrates did not allow his astonishment to appear; he contented himself with praising the senate and the people of Abdera very much for taking so great an interest in a fellow-citizen like Democritus as to make the state of his health a public affair. " Lunacy," said he with great seriousness, " is a point at which the greatest philosophers and the greatest idiots meet together; we shall examine into it."

Thrasyllus invited the doctor to dine with him, and was so polite as to have the most distinguished men and the prettiest women in the city to meet him; but Hippocrates, who was short-sighted and wore no spectacles,* did not

* To those who may wonder at this, the notice may be useful, that in those times spectacles had not been invented.

perceive the loveliness of the latter, and hence
it happened, without its being the fault of the
good creatures, who had adorned themselves for
the occasion to the utmost, that they did not
make the impression upon him which might have
been expected. It was really a pity that he
could not see better. The sight of a beautiful
woman is always agreeable to a sensible man,
and should she say anything stupid, which will
happen sometimes to a pretty woman as well as
to an ugly one, it makes a marked difference if
she is not only listened to, but looked at. In
the latter case, we are always inclined to see, in
all that she says, only what is sensible and
polite, or at least supportable. As the Abderite ladies lost this advantage with the short-
sighted foreigner, and as he was obliged to
judge of their beauty by the impression they
made on his ears, the idea he formed was
very like that which a deaf man with two excellent eyes might form about the merits of a
concert.

"Who is the lady who just now spoke to that
witty gentleman?" asked he, in a low tone, of
Thrasyllus. The wife of a magnate of the republic was named to him; he looked at her
with great attention. "Confound it!" thought

he to himself, "I cannot get out of my head that visage of an oyster-woman whom I lately heard joking with a Molossian ass-driver, in front of my house."

Thrasyllus had secret intentions respecting our Æsculapius. The dinner was good, his wines seductive, and besides, he commanded the attendance of some Milesian dancing-girls. But Hippocrates ate very little, drank only water, and had seen far better dancing in the house of Aspasia at Athens. He was not to be caught thus. The wise man found there what perhaps he had not found for many years —he felt *ennui*, and he thought it not worth while to hide it from the Abderites.

The Abderites perceived, without any great effort of penetration, what he took care they should see distinctly enough, and of course the remarks that they made upon him were not much to his advantage. "He is profoundly learned," whispered they to each other; "pity that he does not know more of the world!" "All that I know is, that it will never occur to me to fall in love with him," said the pretty Thrysallis.

Meanwhile Thrasyllus made reflections of another kind. "Great man as is Hippocrates, he must have his weak side. He seemed not to care very much about the honours with which the senate overloaded him, nor is he very fond of pleasure; but I will bet that a purse of shining new darics will drive away his sour looks."

As soon as the cloth was removed, Thrasyllus began his task; he took the doctor aside, and endeavoured, while admitting the very great interest he felt in his cousin, to prove that the disorder of his mind was a thing so decided and notorious that nothing but the duty of accomplishing all the formalities of the law would have induced the senate to seek confirmation by a foreign physician of a fact which nobody could doubt. "But as it has occasioned you a great deal of trouble to take the journey, which probably you would not have done without this invitation, nothing can be more just than that you should be indemnified for the loss occasioned you in your professional business by attending here, and that by the person who is most interested in the case; accept, therefore, this trifle as a token of my gratitude, of which I hope to give you further proofs."

A pretty round purse, which Thrasyllus pressed into the hand of the physician as he uttered these words, awoke him from the abstraction with which he had listened to the speech of the senator.

"What am I to do with this purse?" asked Hippocrates, with a phlegm that quite disconcerted the Abderite; "you certainly meant to give it to your steward. Are you often subject to such fits of absence?—if such be the case, I would advise you to speak to your physician. But you have reminded me why I am here, and I thank you for so doing; my stay must be a short one, and I cannot delay any longer the visit which, as you know, I owe to Democritus."

With these words the Æsculapius made his bow and disappeared.

The senator never looked so foolish as at this moment, for how could an Abderite legislator imagine that such a thing could ever happen?

There are accidents for which we cannot always be prepared.

CHAPTER VI.

Hippocrates pays a visit to Democritus.—Secret history
of the ancient Order of Cosmopolites.

Hippocrates, as history says, found our naturalist occupied in dismembering different animals, studying their inner conformation, and
the animal economy generally, in order to discover the causes of certain differences in their
qualities and vocations.

This occupation furnished them with a rich
subject for conversation, which left Democritus
but a short time in uncertainty as to the identity
of the foreigner. Their reciprocal pleasure at
such an unexpected meeting was equal to the
magnitude of their respective qualities; but
on the part of Democritus it was so much the
more lively from his having been living for so
long a period remote from the society of students
like himself.

There is a kind of mortals, of whom mention

has been made by the ancients under the name
of Cosmopolites, and who, without any mutual
agreement, without orders, without lodges, and
without the obligation of an oath, constituted a
sort of brotherhood, and kept better united than
any other order in the world. Two such cosmopolites might come, one from the east, and the
other from the west, see each other for the first
time, and at once become friends; not by a secret
sympathy, which is, perhaps, only to be found in
romances; not because duty or oaths forced
them to it; no, but because they were *cosmopolites*. In every other order false brethren, or
at least unworthy ones, are to be found, but in
this order of cosmopolites it was an impossibility; and I think this no small advantage of
the cosmopolites above all other societies, com-
munities, corporations, orders, and brotherhoods
in the world, among which where is there one
that could boast of never having had ambitious,
envious, avaricious, censorious, calumniating,
boasting, hypocritical, double-dealing, back-
biting, ungrateful, ill-intentioned members, or
of not ranking among its numbers a single flat-
terer, parasite, and slave,—a single pedant,
false prophet, and buffoon? The cosmopolites
alone could make this boast.

Their society did not exclude the impure by mysterious ceremonies or terrifying ordeals, as did formerly the Egyptian priests ; these were excluded by themselves, and it is just as difficult to make false pretensions to the character of a cosmopolite as to that of a vocalist or violinist : the deception would have been discovered as soon as attempted. It was impossible to imitate the mode of thinking peculiar to the cosmopolites, their principles, opinions, language, temper, warmth of heart, or even their caprices, faults, and failings, because it was a veritable secret to all who did not belong to their order,—not a secret depending on the discretion of the members, or on their caution not to be overheard, but a secret over which Nature herself has thrown a veil. The cosmopolites might, without hesitation, proclaim it with trumpets throughout the world, being certain that no one but themselves could comprehend it. Under such circumstances it is natural that mutual agreement and confidence should be established between cosmopolites in the first hour of their acquaintance. Pylades and Orestes were not better friends after twenty years of trial and sacrifice together, than were these from the first moment that they

recognized each other. Their friendship required
not to be advanced by time to maturity; it
needed no such trial, it was founded on the firs
law of nature, in the disposition to gratify ou₁
own self-love by a love towards those who are
the most like ourselves.

It would be asking from us something impossible, if not absurd, to be more explicit about
the mysteries of these cosmopolites, because,
as we have said clearly enough to be understood,
it belongs to the nature of the thing, that to the
outer world it would be an enigma to which
none save the members of the order could
furnish the key. The only information we can
add, is, that their number was in all times very
small, and that, notwithstanding the invisibility
of their society, they had an influence on the
affairs of the world, whose effect was the more sure
and durable, as it was attained very quietly, and
by means which served to turn aside the observation of the multitude. To the man who finds
this a new riddle, we counsel rather to dismiss
the subject than needlessly to puzzle his brains
about a matter which concerns him so little.

Democritus and Hippocrates both belonged to
this wonderful and rare order of men. They
had been for a long time, although without

being aware of the fact, the most intimate of
friends ; and their meeting had more the appearance of rejoining each other after a long separa-
tion, than of a new and growing acquaintance.

Their conversations, about which the reader
is, perhaps, curious, were certainly interesting
enough to merit publicity; but to relate them
would carry us too far from the Abderites, who are
the avowed objects of this story. All we can say
about it is, that our cosmopolites spent the
whole evening and greater part of the night in
a conference for which the time was only too
brief, and that they forgot their antipodes, the
Abderites and their senate, as well as the
reasons for which Hippocrates had been sent,
just as much as if such people and such objects
had never existed.

It was only on the following morning, when,
after a long sleep of a few hours, they met
together to enjoy the morning air on a hill
bordering the gardens of Democritus, that the
view of the town, lying before them in the sun-
shine, reminded Hippocrates that he had business in Abdera.   " Can you guess," said he to
his friend, " for what purpose the Abderites
have invited me ? "

" The *Abderites* have invited you ? " cried

Democritus; "I have not heard just now of pestilence raging amongst them. There is, indeed, an hereditary disease which they all and sundry, with but very few exceptions, suffer from; but——"

"You have hit it, Democritus! you have hit it! That is the very thing."

"You are jesting," replied Democritus. "Is it possible that the Abderites have an idea of what they are deficient in? I know them too well; their malady lies chiefly in the fact that they never feel it."

"Yet nothing is more certain," replied Hippocrates, "than that I should not have come to Abdera, had not the Abderites been tormented with the same evil of which you are speaking,— the poor creatures!"

"Ah! I understand you now," replied the philosopher; "your calling here is in consequence of their malady, without their being aware of it. Let me see—ah! I have it!—I'll wager all the world they have brought you here to prescribe as much blood-letting and hellebore to the honest Democritus as he can bear, in order to make him a little more like them. Is it not so?"

"You know your people perfectly well, as I perceive, Democritus, and in fact it requires a very practical and experimental knowledge of their folly to speak so coolly about it."

"Just as if there were not Abderites everywhere!" said the philosopher.

"But Abderites of so high a degree! Pardon me if I cannot judge your fatherland with so much indulgence as you do; but meanwhile, depend upon it, they have not called me in for nothing."

CHAPTER VII.

Hippocrates prescribes for the Abderites.—Great and dangerous commotions which occur upon this in the great councils, and how, fortunately for the Abderite republic, the watchman all at once reduces everything to order.

THE time arrived when the physician was to deliver his report to the senate. He came, stepped into the midst of the assembled fathers, and spoke with an eloquence which stupefied his auditors.

"Peace be with Abdera! noble, firm, far-sighted, and wise lords and Abderites. Yesterday I applauded you for your solicitude concerning the health of Democritus. To-day I advise you to extend that solicitude to the whole of your town and republic. To be sound in body and mind is the highest good you can procure for yourselves, your countrymen, and your children; and to insure this is your first official duty. Short as my stay has been here, it has been long enough to convince me that the Abderites are not in so sound a state as might be wished. It is true I was born at Cos, and reside sometimes in Athens, sometimes in Larissa, and oftentimes elsewhere—to-day I am in Abdera, I shall, perhaps, be to-morrow on my way to Byzantium;—but I am not a Coan, neither an Athenian, nor a Larissian, nor an Abderite. I am a physician : as long as there are sick people on the earth, my duty is to restore health to as many as I can. The most dangerously sick are those who are least aware of being so, and this is the case with the Abderites ; the evil lies too deep for my art, and all I can do towards healing is, to advise you to send with the first favourable breeze six great ships to Anticyra. I do not care with what sort of a freight the Abderites may choose to load them outward, but on arriving at Anticyra let them be laden with as much hellebore as they will bear without sinking. Hellebore can be got from Galatia also, which is a little cheaper, but that from Anticyra is the best. At the return of the ships, assemble all the people in your great forum, make a solemn procession to all your temples, headed by your clergy, and implore the

gods to grant the senate and people of Abdera
that of which they are most in want. Afterwards
you shall return to the forum, and divide your
stock of hellebore amongst all the citizens, at
the cost of the republic, to the extent of seven
pounds *per* head. Do not forget to present the
senators with a double quantity, who, besides
what they require for themselves, have to find
understanding for so many others. The dose is
a strong one, I confess, but inveterate evils are
stubborn, and can be subdued only by a perse-
vering use of medicine. After you have used
for the requisite time this preparatory means,
according to the prescription which I will give
you, then I will hand you over to another physician, because, as I told you, the disease of the
Abderites lies too deep for my skill. I know
only one man within fifty miles of Abdera who
could radically relieve you, if you would follow
patiently and perseveringly his advice. That
man is called Democritus, son of Damasippus.
Do not be prevented by the circumstance of
his having been born in Abdera, for he is not
an Abderite, I assure you; but if you will not
believe me, then ask the oracle of Apollo at
Delphi,—he is a good-hearted deity, and will
feel pleasure in offering you his services,

and herewith I commend you and your city
to the gods. Gentlemen and citizens of Abdera,
do not despise my advice because it costs you
nothing; it is the best I have ever given to the
sick who believe themselves healthy." With
these words Hippocrates took his leave of the
senate and went his way.

"Never," says the historian Hecatæus (a witness all the more trustworthy because he was
himself an Abderite),* "were two hundred
gentlemen seen sitting in so strange an attitude
as were the members of the Abderite council at
that moment, excepting, perhaps, the two hundred Phœnicians who were changed by Perseus
into as many statues by means of a glance at
the head of Medusa, when their leader Phineus
attempted to take violently away from him his
dearly-loved and dearly-won Andromeda;" † in
fact, they had all the reason in the world to be
petrified for several minutes. It would be lost
labour to describe what feelings passed within
their bosoms, because nothing passed there at

* Unfortunately all his works have been lost. See
Recherches sur Hécatée de Milet, tom ix.: des mém.
de Littérat.

† Ovid, Metamorph., t. v., p. 218.

all — their minds were as petrified as their bodies.

With silent stupor they looked towards the door by which the physician had retired, and in every countenance might be seen an immense effort to understand the whole occurrence, and at the same time an utter impossibility of so doing. Finally, but by slow degrees, they seemed to recover, some sooner, some later. They looked at each other with dilated eyes; fifty mouths opened at once to ask the same question, and closed again, because they had opened before knowing what they had to say.

"I'll be hanged," exclaimed at last the Alderman Pfrieme, " if the quack has not been making fools of us, with his rations of helle-bore."

"I expected from the beginning nothing good could come from him," said Thrasyllus.

"He did not particularly please my wife yesterday," added the senator Smilax.

"I thought at once things would not turn out right, when he began to talk of the six vessels that we were to send to Anticyra," said another.

"And the confounded gravity with which he

did it all!" cried a fourth. " I must confess I had not the slightest idea what he was driving at."

" Ha! ha! ha! a very ridiculous affair, as I'm an honest man!" said the stout little senator, holding both his sides. " We must own that we have been fairly taken in—a decided knock-down blow; such ought never to have fallen upon us. Ha! ha! ha!"

" But who ever could have supposed it, from such a man?" shouted the nomophylax.

" To be sure, he is one of your philosophers," said Alderman Pfrieme; " the priest Strobylus is really not so far wrong. If it were not against our liberties, I should be the first to propose that we hunt all such rogues out of our country."

" Gentlemen," began the archon, " the honour of the city of Abdera is attacked, and, instead of sitting here wondering and making idle observations, we ought to think earnestly what is to be done in such a ticklish position. Before all, let us see whether Hippocrates has really gone."

An officer, who was sent to inquire, brought back the intelligence that he was nowhere to be found.

"A most abominable trick," cried the senators, with one voice, "if he has escaped us!"

"Suppose he should be a sorcerer," said the chief of the cordwainers' corporation, searching after an amulet which he used to carry about him as a security against malignant spirits and the evil eye.

Soon came the report that the foreign gentleman had been seen riding quietly on his mule behind the temple of the Dioscuri, on the road to the country-house of Democritus.

"What is to be done now, gentlemen?" said the archon.

"Yes, indeed! What is to be done? What *is* to be done? That is the question," said the members, appealing to each other.

After a long pause it was clear that the gentlemen did not know what was to be done.

"The man is held in great respect by the King of Macedonia," continued the archon; "he is looked upon in all Greece as a second Æsculapius. We shall place ourselves in a very awkward position if we give way, however justly, to our indignation against so great a man. For my part, I only care for the honour of Abdera."

"Pardon me, Master Archon," interrupted Alderman Pfrieme. "No one can be more jealous for the honour and freedom of Abdera than myself, but after due reflection I cannot see how the honour of the State is compromised in this occurrence. This Harpocrates, or Hippocrates as he calls himself, is a doctor, and I have always heard that a physician looks upon the world as a vast hospital, and considers all men as his patients. Everybody speaks and acts according to his understanding, and everybody believes easily enough what he wishes to believe. Hippocrates would certainly be pleased, I think, to see us all sick, in order to have the more patients to attend. ' Well,' thinks he, ' if I can induce them to take my medicines they will become sick enough.' My name is not Pfrieme if this be not the whole secret."

"Upon my soul, so it is—neither more nor less!" cried the stout little alderman. "The fellow is not so foolish, after all. I guess that if he can, he will bring upon us all possible fluxes and fevers, only to have the job of making us well again, and to get a few fees. Ha! ha! ha!"

"But fourteen pounds of hellebore for every senator!" cried one of the oldest, whose brain, judging from his appearance, was certainly quite dry enough. "By all the frogs, it is too bad! It is easy to see that something more lies behind it."

"Fourteen pounds of hellebore for every senator!" repeated the alderman, and laughed loudly.

"And for every head of a guild," added Smilax, with a significant glance.

"I beg your pardon; he did not say a word about the heads of companies," cried Alderman Pfrieme.

"But it is, of course, understood," replied the other,—"senators, aldermen, and common-councilmen. Aldermen and senators, I do not see why the common council ought to be excepted."

"What! how!" cried Alderman Pfrieme, with great energy. "You don't see that? Gentlemen, you heard it all! Mr. Town-clerk, please make a note of it in the proceedings."

All the common-councilmen rose at once from their seats, grumbling.

"Did I not say," said the hypochondriacal alderman, "that there was something more behind the scenes? A secret attempt is designed against the aristocracy; but those gentlemen have betrayed themselves too soon."

"Against the aristocracy!" cried Pfrieme, in a still louder tone. "Against what aristocracy?"

"By Jove! Mr. Alderman, at what period was Abdera ever an aristocracy? Are we aldermen and common-councilmen here only as figures painted on a wall? Do we not represent the people? Have we not to defend our laws and our liberties? Mr. Town-clerk, I protest against everything to the contrary in the name of the respectable body of common-councilmen in the republic of Abdera."

"We protest! we all protest!" cried the common-councilmen.

"We re-protest! we re-protest!" cried the senators.

The uproar became tremendous.

"Gentlemen!" cried the reigning archon, as loud as he could, "what hallucination has taken possession of you? Pray remember who you are, and where you are. What will the butter-women and greengrocers down below think, if they hear us crying out as if we were having our teeth drawn?"

But the voice of reason could not be heard amid the stunning hubbub. No one could hear himself speak.

Fortunately, from remotest time it had been the practice throughout Abdera to dine precisely at twelve o'clock; and according to an order of council, a sort of herald, as soon as that hour had passed, stepped before the town-hall and proclaimed the time.

" Honourable gentlemen !" shouted the herald, with a voice like that of the Homeric Stentor, " the twelfth hour has passed !"

" Silence ! there is the herald ! What did he say ?"

" The twelfth hour, gentlemen, the twelfth has passed."

" Twelve, already ?"

" Already struck."

" Now there is no time to lose."

The greater number of these gentlemen were to be guests at a great dinner.

The blessed word *twelve* raised at once a succession of ideas of the pleasantest kind, and which ideas had nothing to do with the subject of the quarrel. Quicker than the figures in a raree-show, before each rose up the vision of a huge table covered with numerous dishes, their foreheads became smooth, their noses anticipated the odour of the finest *entrées*, their ears heard the clatter of knives, forks, and plates, their palates tasted already those delicious soups in the invention of which the cooks of Abdera emulated each other. In short, the imaginary banquet occupied the thoughts of all, and tranquillity was at once restored in the Abderite council.

" Where are you to dine to-day ?"

" With Polypontes."

"I am invited there too."

"I am delighted that we are to have the pleasure of your company."

"You do me much honour."

"What play will they give us this evening?"

"The Andromeda of Euripides."

"Well, indeed, that *is* a tragedy."

"Oh, it is my favourite piece."

"And what music?"

"I will tell you confidentially that our nomophylax has himself composed several choruses; you will hear wonders."

With such pleasant discourses the fathers of Abdera arose and left the town-hall, an eager, but peaceful crowd, to the great astonishment of the butter-women, cheesemongers, and greengrocers, who but a moment before had heard the walls resound with a genuine Thracian tumult.

All this was your doing, benevolent timekeeper. Without your assistance, the quarrel between senators and common councilmen, like the anger of Achilles, ridiculous as it was in its origin, would have burst into a flame, and led to the greatest disturbance, if not even to the downfall of the republic.

If ever an Abderite deserved to be rewarded with a public statue, it certainly was this herald.

It may be said that the great service he had rendered to his country loses all its merit from the circumstance that he was only accidentally useful. The worthy man little thought in mechanically calling the stated hour what mischief he was warding off the commonwealth. But it must be remembered that, from time immemorial, no Abderite has merited well of his country in any other way. It had always happened that if anything was done that proved by chance useful to the State, they thanked the gods for it, as though they felt that they were only instruments acting unconsciously and from causes over which they had no control. Meanwhile they took upon themselves the merit of the act, or, to speak more accurately, they allowed it to be attributed to themselves, just as a donkey-driver pockets the daily earnings of his donkeys, and reckons it as much due to his own exertions.

Be it understood that this is only said in reference to the archons, senators, and common-councilmen, because the worthy time-keeper, however much or however little he might serve the republic, got his sixpence a day in good Abderite money, and was thankful.

BOOK III.

EURIPIDES AMONG THE ABDERITES.

———◆———

CHAPTER I.

The Abderites make preparation for going to the theatre.

THE senators of Abdera had an old custom or habit of recounting all the discussions of the council at the dinner-table, whether with company present, or only in their family circle, making them serve as a foundation for witty observations and sportive remarks, or of patriotic groans, complaints, wishes, dreams, and expectations; and this especially just when the greatest discretion was required in the matter. But at that time, although the adventure of the Abderites with the Prince of Physicians was strange enough to have deserved a place in the annals of the republic, yet at all tables where sat

a senator or common-councilman, Hippocrates
and Democritus were as little thought of, or
talked about, as if no such persons were in existence.   In this matter the Abderites showed
themselves possessed of proper " public spirit,"
and a much finer sense of propriety than could
be expected from them, considering their ob-
stinacy.   In fact, their story with Hippocrates,
let them turn it and colour it as they might,
was not to be told in any way that could do
them honour; and the wisest way of treating
such a subject was exactly what they did—they
let it drop, and said nothing.

The play for the evening constituted at this
time, as usual, one of the chief topics of discourse at their entertainment.   As the Abderites, following the example of their models,
the Athenians, had provided themselves with
their own theatre, so in all their parties, as soon
as the usual subjects of the weather, fashion,
news of the day, and scandal were exhausted,
they began to talk of the play which was performed yesterday, or of that which was to be
acted to-day; and the gentlemen of Abdera
congratulated themselves, especially before foreigners, that it afforded their countrymen and
countrywomen a nice opportunity for perfecting

their wit and taste, that it supplied them with
an inexhaustible source of innocent conversation
in society, and that it was invaluable to the fair
sex as affording an excellent remedy against *ennui*,
which was so destructive to the body and the
mind. We do not say it in order to blame, but
on the contrary in order to praise the Abderites,
that they attached such importance to their theatre as to appoint a committee of the council to
watch over it, whose president was always the
nomophylax for the time, and consequently one
of the first magnates of the place. This was in-
contestably praiseworthy : all that could be said
against the arrangement was, that the affairs
of their drama were none the better for it,—
at the same time, this was no more than in
Abdera might reasonably be expected. For
as the choice of the pieces depended on this
committee, and as the invention of play-
bills belongs to the numerous class which
establish the superiority of modern times over
old ones, so it generally happened that the
public knew nothing of what was to be performed, and this especially if a new author
wished to produce a piece on the stage : the
gentlemen of the committee did not make any
secret of the thing, but it had nevertheless to

pass through so many wry mouths, and so many obtuse ears, that it almost always came out a *quid pro quo ;* and the audience, if they, for instance, had been expecting the Antigone of Sophocles, were obliged to be content with the Erigone of Physignathus—as, indeed, they almost always were. " What are you about to give us to-day? " was the general question in Abdera,—a question which, in itself, was the most innocent in the world, but which yet, through one little circumstance, became truly Abderitish : this was because the answer could not be of any practical use, for the people always went to the play, whether the piece was old or new, good or bad. Properly speaking, there were no *bad* pieces for the *Abderites,* because they accepted everything as good ; and a natural consequence of this unbounded good-nature was, that there were no *good* pieces for them. Bad or good, if they were amused, all was right, and anything looking like a play did amuse them.

Every piece, however miserably deficient and badly performed, terminated amidst applause, which seemed as though it would never leave off; and when the question ran through the theatre—"Have you been pleased with the play ?"—the invariable reply was, " Yes, indeed."

However inclined our readers may be to look
without wonder on any of the peculiarities of
this Thracian Athens, yet the fact just related
is so strange that it can hardly claim belief
without some explanation. That the Abderites,
with all their taste for the drama, should have
brought themselves to so complete a state of
apathy, or rather indifference, that a bad piece
should not only occasion them no displeasure,
but should be as acceptable to them, or nearly
so, as a good one, is almost too much for credence.

We must take advantage of the need of solv-
ing this riddle to make a digression on the
whole history of the drama among the Abderites; but before this we must ask the reasonable and right-thinking reader a little favour, the
granting of which will in the end be a matter of
more advantage to him than to ourselves, and
this is, in spite of inward suggestions to the
contrary, not to imagine that we allude, under
feigned names, to the dramatic authors, the
actors, or the audience of his beloved fatherland. It is true, and we do not deny it, that
all the Abderite story, to a certain extent, has
a double meaning; but without the key to this
secret intention, which our readers must obtain

from ourselves, they would every moment be in danger of making false interpretations. Till then we must ask them,

" Per genium, dextrámque, Deosque Penates,"

to avoid making any ungenerous or unfriendly application, and in all that follows, as well as throughout the book, not to read in a different state of mind from that in which they would read any other old or new, but impartial, historical relation.

CHAPTER II.

Exacter notices concerning the Abderite national theatre.—Taste of the Abderites.—Character of the nomophylax Gryllus.

When the Abderites resolved to have a permanent theatre, it was decided, from patriotic feelings, that it should be a national one. Now, as the nation, at least the majority, consisted of Abderites, their theatre was necessarily an Abderite one, and this was the first and irremediable cause of all sorts of evil.

The respect which the Abderites professed for the holy city of Minerva, as their reputed mother, involved as a necessary consequence that all Athenian dramas should be held in high estimation, not merely because they were good, which indeed was not always the case, but because they came from Athens. At first, for want of a sufficient number of home-made pieces, scarcely anything else was represented ; but just for this reason, not only for the honour of the town and republic of Abdera, but for several other motives, it was thought necessary to erect in the midst of their own city a manufactory of comedies and tragedies, and to encourage by all possible means this poetry-spinning, by means of which all the Abderite wit, feelings, customs, and follies, as so many rough natural products, should be dramatically worked up for their own use, as was becoming to good and wise rulers and patriots.   To do this out of the public chest was impossible, for two reasons—first, because there was very little in it, and secondly at that time it was not the fashion to make the spectators pay, but the State was obliged to defray the cost, and had outlay sufficient without this addition.   To tax the inhabitants further without knowing beforehand how they would relish this new amusement or not, was a thing not to be imagined.   There remained no other way than that of encouraging Abderite authors at the expense of the common taste, and the authorities therefore accepted as good every production that was tendered gratis, following the old proverb, " not to look a gift horse in the mouth," or, as the Abderites used to

say, " When there is eating for nothing there is
always good cooking."

What Horace says about Rome in his time—

" Scribimus indocti doctique poemata passim"—

might be said in a superlative sense of the Abderites.   It was considered a meritorious thing to
write a play, and in so doing there was really
nothing to risk. Everybody wrote tragedies who
had only wit enough to string together some
score of thoughts in an equal number of bombas-
tic periods, and every common jester tried his
hand at exposing on the stage the failings of the
Abderites, of which he in society and at public
places set forth a manifest example in himself.

This patriotic toleration of national productions
had the effect of increasing the evil and render-
ing it permanent.

However thoughtless, boastful, silly, unprinci-
pled, ignorant, and idle, the young patricians
were in Abdera, one or other of them was
perpetually prevailed on by his favourite, his
parasite, or his own hereditary stupidity, to
imagine that he could earn dramatic laurels as
well as another; and his first essay was always
crowned with so much success, that Blemmias,
nephew of the archon Onolaus, a youth of

seventeen and (a thing not uncommon in the family) a notorious simpleton, felt an unaccountable itching in his fingers to write a *goat-play*, as at that time the thing was called to which the name of *tragedy* is now applied.

Never since Abdera stood on Thracian ground, never was seen a more stupid native production ; but the author was a nephew of the archon, and therefore he could not fail. The pit, or arena, was so crowded that young gentlemen were obliged to take upon their knees the loveliest of the Abderite beauties. The common people stood on each other's shoulders. The five acts were listened to in stupid, unbroken silence. There were yawning, sighing, wiping of the forehead, rubbing of the eyes, and unspeakable weariness ; but it *was* listened to, and when the long-desired conclusion arrived, it was greeted with such thunders of applause that several rather delicate and nervous gentlemen lost their hearing altogether.

Now it is quite clear that it was not so very difficult to write a tragedy, since the young Blemmias had achieved one. Everybody, without great presumption, might suppose himself equal to the task; so it became a point of honour that every respectable family should boast of at

least one son or nephew, or brother-in-law, or
other relative, who had bequeathed a goat-play
or a comedy to the national stage, or at least an
opera. It was not thought necessary to inquire
into the real merits of the piece; good, indifferent,
and bad, ran together in the same category. No
cabal was necessary to uphold a bad piece—one
politeness answered to another; and as the gentlemen were all in the same predicament, nobody
bethought himself of whispering to his neighbour
that "King Midas had the ears of an ass."

It is easy to comprehend that the dramatic
art could not gain much by this tolerance; but
why should the Abderites trouble themselves
about the interests of the art? It was sufficient
that similar productions passed off quietly, to the
tranquillity of the State and the general amusement of the interested parties. "It may thus
be seen," the archon would say, "how important it is to take a thing by its right end.
Dramatic affairs, which are almost always giving
rise to the most shameful quarrels in Athens,
become in Abdera a bond of union and a source
of the most innocent pastime in the world,
People go to the play, amuse themselves in one
way or another, either listening to it, or in
conversation, or in sleeping, as the case may be.

Afterwards comes the applause, and everybody goes home satisfied; and then, ' Good night !' "

We have already mentioned that the Abderites were so occupied with their theatre, that it was nearly the only subject of conversation in their parties, and so it was; but if they talked of dramatic pieces, or performances, or actors, it was not to examine what ought to be applauded or otherwise, because they made it depend upon their own will or caprice whether a thing were good or not, and, as has been remarked, they had come to a mutual though tacit agreement to encourage their homebred national dramatic manufacture.

" It is clearly perceptible," said they, " how important are the results where the arts are encouraged. But twenty years ago we had only two or three poets, who, except on birthdays or weddings, are not noticed by anybody now; within the twelve years that we have had our own theatre, we can produce more than six hundred pieces, great and small together, which sprang up on Abderite ground."

When they conversed of their plays, it was only to question each other thus :—" Whether yesterday's piece were not pretty;" and to reply thus :—" Yes, it was very nice; and what a

beautiful dress the actress wore who personated
Iphigenia, or Andromeda!"—because in Abdera the female characters were represented by
women (not so Abderitish a custom after all),
and this served as a foundation for thousands of
interesting observations, discourses, and replies,
upon the dress, voice, demeanour, motion, car-
riage of the head, and twenty other things
of the same kind. In the same way they
talked of the operas, as well of the music as
of the "words": such was the term applied
to the poetry. One stated what it was that
had pleased him best; the most sublime and
stirring passages were discussed; there was fault
found here and there with a low expression
or exaggerated sentiment, but the critic always
finished with the eternal Abderite chorus, "It
was nevertheless a pretty piece;" while the
short stout senator would occasionally add,—
"And it contains a very good moral—a beautiful
moral;"—only it happened unfortunately that the
pieces which he praised for their morality were
generally the worst of all.

It will be thought, perhaps, the special reason
why pieces of home manufacture were so much
encouraged in Abdera, without regard to merit
or quality, did not apply to foreign ones; that

the great difference among the Athenian dra
matic authors, and the distance at which an
Acydamus stood from a Sophocles, might have
served to form the taste of the Abderites, and
enabled them to distinguish between the bad and
the good, the excellent and the barely tolerable;
above all, between a powerful and natural genius
and mere pretensions and apish imitation, between the equal, regular march of a true master,
and the stilted steps of an imitator. But, in the
first place, taste cannot be acquired without a
certain delicacy of that organ of the mind
(perception) by which it must be tested, and
which, we have already observed at the com-
mencement of this story, nature seemed to have
altogether refused to the Abderites. To them
everything was good; on their tables might be
found the masterpieces of wit and genius, together with the commonplaces of the most
wretched bunglers. They could be imposed upon
in every way, and nothing was more easy than
to palm upon an Abderite the sublimest ode
of Pindar as the attempt of a beginner, and,
on the contrary, the most nonsensical scribbling
in the shape of a song, with strophe and anti-
strophe, for the work of Pindar. For this
reason, the same question was asked concern-

ing every new drama which was placed before them, "By whom?"—and there were a thousand instances of their remaining indifferent to a most excellent work, until they learned that it was connected with a celebrated name.

It must be added that the nomophylax Gryllus, son of Cyniscus, who took the leading part in the erection of the Abderite national theatre, and was the head inspector of their theatrical board, thought himself a great *connoisseur* in music, and the first composer of his time,—a claim against which the Abderites had nothing to say, as he was a very popular man, and all his compositions consisted of melodies which could be adapted to every kind of text, and consequently nothing could be more easy than to sing and commit them to memory. Facility in composing was the quality of which Gryllus was especially proud.

"Well, how do you like my Iphigenia, Hecuba, Alcestis (or whatever else it was), eh?"

"Oh! delightful! Mr. Nomophylax—admirable! It is a pure composition, flowing, melodious."

"And how long do you think I have worked at it?—do count, please. To-day is the 13th; on the 4th, at five o'clock (you know I am an

early riser), I sat down to my desk, and yesterday, exactly at ten o'clock in the morning, I
put the finishing stroke to it.   Well, now, do
reckon:—4th, 5th, 6th, 7th, 8th, 9th, 10th, 11th,
12th—it makes out, as you see, not quite nine
full days, and among them two council-days,
and two or three in which I had dinner en-
gagements, without taking into account other
business.   Hem! what say you to that ?—is it
not smart work? I do not mention it for praise,
but I am satisfied that, for a wager, no composer
in European or Asiatic Greece could be prepared
with a piece sooner than myself.   That is
nothing—but it is my own peculiar talent,
eh?"

We expect our readers can see the man before them, and if they have any talent for
music they will comprehend his Iphigenia, Alcestis, or Hecuba, as well as though he had
played them all through on a hand-organ.
But, besides this little weakness, this great man
was possessed with the idea that the only good
music to be found was his own.   Not one of the
best composers of Athens, Thebes, Corinth, &c.,
&c., could come near him, in his own opinion;
even Damon himself, whose graceful, spirited,
and heart-stirring productions bewitched every

one who had any soul (except in Abdera)—
even Damon was described by him as a street-
singers' composer. With this mode of thinking,
and by the infinite facility with which he
poured forth his musical inspirations, he had
within a few years set to music more than sixty
pieces of the Athenian drama, celebrated or un-
celebrated; he left the Abderite national pieces
mostly to his pupils and imitators, and contented himself with giving the finishing touch
to their work. It is true that his choice, as
may be imagined, fell not always on the best
dramas. Most of those he selected were bom-
bastic caricatures of Æschylus, common farces,
or show-pieces which were intended by their
authors for the amusement of the lowest of the
populace. But it was enough that the nomophylax, a chief man of the State, had composed
the music: they were infinitely applauded, and
though, by their frequent repetition, the jaws
of the audience were almost dislocated with
yawning, yet they never failed to assure each
other, on going out of the theatre, that it was
indeed a beautiful play, and delightful music.

And thus everything combined to produce
an indifference, not only as to the variety and
shades of beauty, but as to the positively good

L 2

or bad, by which, as a strong national characteristic, these Thracian Athenians distinguished
themselves from all other polished nations of the
earth,—an indifference which was the more remarkable, as it still left them the faculty of
being struck in a very strange way by the really
beautiful, as will be seen shortly by a remarkable example.

CHAPTER III.

Contributions to the literary history of Abdera.—Notice concerning their first dramatic authors, Hyperbolus, Paraspasmus, Antiphilus, and Thlaps.

WITH all this indifference, tolerance, apathy, or whatever we please to call it, we must not imagine that the Abderites were a people wholly devoid of taste : they really possessed their five senses, and notwithstanding that under the above circumstances everything was pleasant to them, they still found that one thing pleased them more than another; so they had their favourite plays and favourite authors, just the same as other people.

At the time that the little vexation about Dr. Hippocrates overtook them, there were amongst the pretty large number of dramatic authors who made a trade of it, without taking

into account the volunteers, two particularly
who possessed the favour of the Abderite public.   One of these wrote tragedies, and a kind
of pieces called comic operas ; the other, whose
name was Thlaps, a sort of intermediate affair,
at which nobody could either laugh or cry,—
dramas which he had the honour of inventing,
for which reason they were called by his admirers *Thlapsodies.*

The first alluded to was Hyperbolus, of
whom it has already been mentioned at the
beginning of this true and delectable history,
that he was the most celebrated author in Abdera.   He was also distinguished in other matters.   The extraordinary partiality of his fellow-citizens for him awarded to him in every
possible way the prize of pre-eminence, which
distinction obtained for him the pompous name
of Hyperbolus, his family name being Hegesias.
The reason that this man found such high favour
with the Abderites, was naturally enough the
very one why he and his works would have
been hissed everywhere else.   He, amongst all
authors, was the one in whom appeared the true
spirit of Abdera, with all its idiotisms, and freedom from the beauties, proportions, and traits
of ordinary human nature.   He was the poet

with whom all his fellow-citizens sympathized the most, who acted always just as they would have done, whose very speeches resembled their own, who always found the very point which would amuse and tickle them—in a word, an author after their minds and hearts; and this not because he possessed any extraordinary sagacity, or because he made this the object of his study, but simply because amongst all his comrades he was the truest Abderite. It might be depended on that the point of view from which he regarded a thing would be the worst, and that he perceived a likeness just where the difference was the most palpable to others; that he always endeavoured to look solemn where a sensible man laughed, and laughed when all but an Abderite would think only of mourning. A man who was so deeply imbued with the Abderitan genius, could of course in Abdera do whatever he liked. He was, too, their Anacreon, their Alcæus, their Pindar, their Æschylus, their Aristophanes, and had lately been working at a grand national epic, in forty-eight books, to be called "*The Abderiad*," to the great joy of the whole Abderite people, "because," said they, "we only want a Homer, and when Hyperbolus is ready with his Abderiad, we shall have in one

piece both the Iliad and the Odyssey; and then
let the other Greeks come and look over our
shoulders, if they dare. They will not attempt
after this to show us a man whose equal could
not be found amongst ourselves."

In the mean time, however, tragedy was the
principal department of Hyperbolus; he had
constructed altogether, large and small, about
a hundred and twenty dramas, a circumstance
which, among a people who judged of all things
by the number and the size, constituted in itself
a reason for their extraordinary preference, because amongst all his rivals not one could exhi-
bit a third part of this number. Notwithstanding that he was called by the Abderites, from the
bombast of his style, their Æschylus, he piqued
himself not a little on his originality. "Point
me out in all my works," said he, "a character,
an idea, a sentiment, an expression, which is
taken from another!"

"Or from nature!" added Democritus.

"Oh! I grant you that," cried Hyperbolus;
"and I do not think I have lost a great deal by
it. Nature! nature!—men are always talking
about this *nature*, without knowing what they
mean. *Human nature* (and that is what you are
speaking of) belongs to comedies, farces, thlap-

sodies, and the like! But tragedy must step
beyond *nature*, or I would not give a fig for
it!" This was the quality of his own works,
and there could be no mistake about it.

No man ever looked like *his* personages, or
spoke, felt, thought, or acted like them; but
then this was just what delighted the Abderites,
and why they esteemed Sophocles less than any
other foreign poet.

"If I might give my opinion frankly," said
Hyperbolus one day in a highly respectable
party, where this subject was discussed in a
truly Abderite manner, "I never could conceive what there is to be found so extraordinary
in the Œdipus or in the Electra of Sophocles,
and especially in his Philoctetes. As a successor
of so sublime an author as Æschylus, he certainly
falls off strangely. As to Attic polish I do not
deny it to him—polish as much as you like!
But where are the flashes of fire, the lightning
thoughts, the thunderbolts, the overwhelming
whirlwind—in short, the giant's strength, the
eagle's flight, the lion-like force, the storms and
hurricanes, which distinguish the true tragic
author—where are they?"

"This may be called speaking of a thing like
a master of the subject," said one of the party.

" Oh! for such matters, you may rely on the judgment of Hyberbolus ! " cried another.

" How should he help understanding it? He has written a hundred and twenty tragedies—he is the dramatic author of Abdera," whispered a fair Abderite to a foreigner.

In the mean time, two among his rivals, pupils, and imitators, succeeded in shaking the tragic throne on which he had been placed by general acclamation :—one by a piece in which the hero, in the first act, murders his father; in the second, he marries his sister; in the third, discovers that she is the offspring of his incestuous intercourse with his own mother; in the fourth, he cuts off his own ears and nose ; and in the fifth, after having poisoned his mother and strangled his sister, he is carried away by the Furies amidst thunder and lightning to Tartarus ;—the other by a Niobe, in which, besides a great amount of " oh, oh's ! " " phew, phew's ! " and "hellellelleleus!" and some blasphemies which make the hair of the hearers stand on end, the whole play is performed in action and pantomime. Both pieces produced the most stupendous effect : never since the existence of Abdera had so many handkerchiefs been steeped in tears as during these three hours.

"No—I cannot bear it any longer!" sobbed the beautiful Abderites.

"The poor prince—how he howled! how he threw himself about! how he writhed!"

"And the speech he made after having cut off his nose!" cried another.

"And the Furies—the Furies!" exclaimed another; "I could not close my eyes for a month after that."

"It was dreadful, I must confess," said a fifth. "But oh! the Niobe! how she stands amidst all her children, piled one upon another, tearing her hair and scattering it over the weltering bodies, then throwing herself upon them, hoping to recall them to life, then again rising in despair, rolling her eyes so wildly, then tearing her bosom and flinging hands full of blood towards the sky, uttering horrible maledictions against heaven! No—I never saw anything more moving. What a man must this Paraspasmus be to have the power to produce such scenes on the stage!"

"Well, as for the power," said the fair Salabanda, "we are not always to conclude from such evidence. I doubt whether Paraspasmus could keep up to all he seems to promise: great braggarts are bad fighters."

The beautiful Salabanda was a woman who did not say such things without a reason. This simple observation influenced the second performance so much, that it did not produce half its former effect, and the author could never recover the blow which Salabanda gave him in the imagination of the Abderite ladies.

In the mean time, he attained the honour, as well as his friend Antiphilus, of having given a new direction to the tragic drama of Abdera, by the discovery of two new modes of representing it, viz. the grisly and the pantomimic, by which means a new arena was opened to the Abderite authors, who were sure to earn laurels, for in fact nothing was more easy than to frighten children, and to make their heroes say —nothing at all.

As human inconsistency becomes satiated with everything, even with what at first pleases it the most, so the Abderites began to feel *ennui* at hearing and admiring every day what had long ceased to amuse them. Just at that time a young author of the name of Thlaps bethought himself of bringing out pieces on the stage which were neither comedies, nor tragedies, nor farces, but living family pictures of Abderites, —in which neither heroes nor gods, but good, respectable, homebred citizens appeared, attending to their every-day town, market-house, and family business, acting and speaking before a respectable audience, just as if they were simply on the stage of their own houses, and as if, besides themselves, no one existed in the world. It was nearly the same kind of play by which Menander subsequently gained so much glory. The difference consisted in this only, that the one brought Athenians, and the other Abderites, upon the stage, and that the one was Menander, and the other Thlaps. His first piece* of this kind was received with so much enthusiasm, that the like was never witnessed before: the worthy Abderites beheld themselves on the stage for the first time without caricature, without stilts, without the lion-skin sceptre or diadem, but in their usual costume, speaking their usual language, living, loving, eating and drinking, pleasing and being pleased, &c., in their real natural fashion and manner—and this is just what gave them so

---

* He called it "Eugamia, or the Fourfold Bride." Eugamia was promised by her father to one, by her mother to another, and by her aunt (on whose fortune she counted) to a third. Finally it appeared that the forward girl had secretly engaged herself to a fourth.

much pleasure. It was to them just as to a young girl is the seeing her face for the first time in a looking-glass—they could not have enough of it. "The Fourfold Bride" was performed fourteen times in succession, and for a long time the Abderites would hear nothing but thlapsodies. Thlaps, to whom composition was not so easy as to the great Hyperbolus, and to the nomophylax Gryllus, could not prepare them fast enough, but as he had given the ton to his fellow-townsmen, rivals were not wanting; all applied themselves to this new variety, and in less than three years all subjects and titles of thlapsodies were so much exhausted, that it was pitiable to see the woful condition of authors, as they panted and perspired to obtain from the mire which so many had spouted before them one single drop of muddy water.

The natural consequence was, that imperceptibly the respective authors regained their proper equilibrium. The Abderites also, who, just like other human beings, possessed a natural taste for variety, soon discovered that it would be better to preserve themselves from *ennui* by a change. Tragedies both grisly and pantomimic, comedies, operas, and farces, again came into vogue. The nomophylax composed the tragedies of Euripides, *i. e.* set them to music, and Hyperbolus renewed his project of becoming the Abderite Homer, partly because he had made up his mind, however unwillingly, to divide the favour of the Abderite pit with Thlaps, and partly because the latter, by his marriage with the daughter of a rich common-councilman, had lately become a very important personage.

CHAPTER IV.

Remarkable instance of political economy of the Abderites.—End of the digression concerning their
theatrical affairs.

BEFORE we quit this digression and continue
our story, it will be necessary to remove a little
doubt which may arise in the mind of our kind
reader from this description of the Abderite
theatre.

It is inconceivable, one might say, how the
budget of Abdera, whose revenue was never
considerable, could meet the exorbitant expenses
of a daily performance at the theatre, presuming
even that the authors gave their services without
fee or reward. And yet, unless something of
this kind had been the case, we can hardly
understand that there should have been in
Abdera so many dramatic authors by profession,
and that the great Hyperbolus himself should

have brought on the stage no fewer than one hundred and twenty plays.

In order not to keep our reader in suspense without necessity, we will at once confess to him that the Abderite dramatists worked by no means for nothing, as the great law, " Thou shalt not muzzle the ox that treadeth out the corn," is a natural law, and its general obligation was felt even by the natives of Abdera ; and though by a special decree the state treasury was not to pay any expenses of the theatre, yet, for the most part, these were defrayed by parsimony in other and more useful departments.

The thing was thus :—as soon as the patrons of the theatre remarked that the Abderites were inflamed with a passion for the drama, and that theatrical representations had become a necessity for them, they set forth to the people, by a representation from the common council, that the treasury was unable to support this addition to its expenses without a new tax, or the suppression of some other expenses. A committee was accordingly appointed, who, after more than sixty sittings, at last presented to the council a project for the regulation of the public theatre, which was thought to be so sound and well devised, that it was at once confirmed as an Abderite law, at a general meeting of the citizens.

It would give us pleasure to place before the eyes of our readers this Abderite masterpiece, if we could suppose they would have patience enough to peruse it; but should any person or corporation, in or out of the holy Roman empire, wish for the communication, we beg of them to make a regular request to that effect, defraying at the same time all the requisite expenses. All we can say here is, that according to this regulation enough money was collected, without oppression towards the public, to entertain the Abderites with plays four times a week, and not only to remunerate authors, actors, and orchestra, but also the honourable deputies and the nomophylax, and besides this to gratify the two lower classes of spectators, at every performance, with a penny loaf each and two dried figs. The only defect in this regulation was, that the gentlemen of the committee, in drawing up the account of the expenses and the profits (which was received by the State with a perfect reliance on its correctness), made a little mistake of about 28,000 drachmas (rather more than £1000 of our money), which would have to be

paid from the public treasury, the destined
funds not being sufficient. It was indeed no
trifling error in reckoning! In the mean time
the gentlemen of Abdera were so accustomed to
go on smoothly, and *bonâ fide*, in the business
of the public treasury, that many years elapsed
before they discovered that this thousand per
annum had been abstracted from their state
purse, more than they had expected. When it was
finally, with great trouble, discovered, the heads
of the republic found it necessary to lay the
affair before the assembled people, and, *pro
formâ*, propose the suppression of the stage.
But the Abderites behaved in this matter as
they would have done had it been intended to
deprive them of fire and water. In short, a law
was enacted, that the sum yearly required
should be taken from the public treasure de-
posited in the Temple of Latona, and that,
in future, he who should be bold enough
to propose the suppression of the stage,
should be declared an enemy to the city of
Abdera.

Now the Abderites, thinking they had settled
all for the best, used to boast before foreigners
that their drama cost eighty talents without
a call upon the citizens. " All arises from a

good regulation," said they, "by which means we have a national theatre which has no equal in the world."

"That is a great truth," said Democritus; "such authors, such performers, such music— and four times a week—for eighty talents! I for my part, have never found such in any place in the world."

After all they had something to show for it, since it was allowed on all hands that their theatre was one of the most elegant in all Greece. It is true that they had been obliged to pledge their revenues to the King of Macedon, to be enabled to build it; but no one could object to this, as the king had consented that the superintendent, secretaries, and collectors, should be all and for ever Abderites.

We apologize for having detained our readers so long with this general notice of the Abderite theatre. It has just struck six o'clock, and we are going directly to the building itself, where they will be pleased to place themselves either beside the short, stout senator, or the priest Strobylus, or the wit Antistrepsiades, or any one of the fair Abderite ladies to whom they were introduced in a former chapter.

CHAPTER V.

The Andromeda of Euripides is performed. — Great
success of the nomophylax, and how the *prima donna*
contributed towards it. — A few remarks upon the other
actors. — The choruses and the decorations.

THE drama which was this evening to be represented was the Andromeda of Euripides,
one of the sixty or seventy works of that poet
of which only a few, with the exception of some
small fragments, have escaped destruction. The
Abderites paid great respect, without knowing
why, to the name of Euripides, and to all
the works that bore it. Several of his tragedies, or dramas as we should properly call
them, had been performed, and were always pronounced exceedingly beautiful. The Andromeda,
one of the newest, was now for the first time
acted on the Abderite stage. The nomophylax

composed the music to it, and (as he whispered pretty loudly in the ears of his friends) had on this occasion surpassed himself. Perhaps the good man had it in his mind to display all his skill at once, and thus the meaning of the worthy Euripides had entirely escaped his attention. Gryllus, however, was satisfied with himself,—unconcerned whether his music changed the text, or the text his music, into nonsense, which was just the point about which the Abderites cared the least. In short it made a great noise, had many sublime and moving passages (as the brothers, relatives, brothers-in-law, clients, and servants of Gryllus affirmed,) and was received with the loudest applause. Not that there were wanting in Abdera men who, having been endowed with more delicate ears than their fellow-citizens, or having heard elsewhere something better, did confess to each other that the nomophylax, with all his pretensions to being an Orpheus, was nothing more than an organ-grinder, whose best works were merely rhapsodies without taste, and almost without sense. These few were even so bold as on one occasion to make known a little of their heterodoxy to the public; but they were so badly received by the admirers of the Gryllian music, as to be obliged to submit to the majority, in order to escape with a whole skin, and *now* these same gentlemen were the persons who in the very worst passages clapped the loudest.

The orchestra did its best to show itself worthy of its chief. " I have given them enough to do," said Gryllus, and he seemed not a little gratified to find that the poor people, by the end of the first act, had not a dry thread upon them.

By the way it must be owned that the orchestra was an institution in which the Abderites could rival all other cities in the world. The first thing which was said about it to any stranger was, that it was one hundred and twenty strong ; and they added with a significant emphasis, " The Athenian orchestra numbers only eighty performers ; but of course with a hundred and twenty it is easy to perform !" Amongst so many, undoubtedly, some skilful men were to be found—at least, men with whom a really good leader could do something ; but such a leader never was and never could be found in Abdera. Besides, how could this assist their musical affairs ? It was evidently decided in the council of the gods, that in the Thracian Athens nothing should be in its right place, nothing answering to its aim, nothing right, nothing forming a complete whole.

Besides, as the performers got very little for their trouble, it was not thought right to ask much from them; and as the public were satisfied with everybody who tried to do his best, as they called it, nobody did try to do his best. The skilful became lazy, and those who were yet but halfway lost the energy, and finally the power to go onward. Why, indeed, should they give themselves the trouble to attain perfection, when they were working for Abderite ears? It is true that the foreigners amongst them had also ears, but they had no voice in the matter, and found it not worth while to find fault with the taste of Abdera, or perhaps they were too polite, or too politic, so to do. The nomophylax, stupid as he was, remarked as well as others that things did not go on so well as they ought; but then he had no taste, or, what came to the same thing, nothing was relished by him which was not cooked by himself; he always missed the right means by which he might have remedied it, and was too lazy and too awkward to communicate with others in a proper manner.

Perhaps he would sometimes submit when,

as it sometimes happened, his organ-grinder did
not please the ears even of the Abderites, to lay
the fault on the orchestra, and assure the ladies
and gentlemen who paid him compliments, that
not a note had been played as he had written it;
but this was only a fire-escape in case of need,
because it might be seen from the contemptuous
manner in which he spoke of other orchestras,
and from the merit which he claimed for that of
the Abderites, that he was as well satisfied with
it, as it was becoming for a patriotic nomophylax
of Abdera to be.

But without mentioning the perfection of the
music of the Andromeda, and of the scenery, it
is a fact, that for a long time no other piece had
given so much satisfaction. The singer who performed the part of Perseus was so tremendously
applauded, that he forgot himself in the midst
of the most striking passage, and finished it
with a bravura out of another opera—one with
which he was perhaps better acquainted than
with the Andromeda. It is true that it was
a comic opera, the Cyclops; but that mat-
tered nothing on the present occasion;—Andromeda—in the scene where, chained to the rock,
abandoned by all her friends, and exposed to
the anger of the Nereids, she is awaiting with

agony the appearance of the monster—was obliged to repeat her monologue three times. The nomophylax could not conceal his delight at such brilliant success; he walked from box to box to collect the tribute of praise which thundered upon him on all sides; and he confessed, in the midst of these assurances, that "it was doing him too much honour, but that he was not so well satisfied with any other of his toys," as he used modestly to call his operas, "as with his Andromeda."

At the same time, in order to do justice to herself and the Abderites, it would have been only fair to admit, that at least half of the success was to be placed to the account of the actress Eucolpis, who, although already the favourite, found opportunities, in the part of Andromeda, to show herself off so advantageously, that the gentlemen, both young and old, of Abdera, could scarcely look at her enough. Indeed, where there was so much to be seen, there was little necessity of listening. Eucolpis was tall and well-made, a little more substantial, it is true, than was required for an Athenian beauty, but in this case, as in many others, the Abderites were decidedly Thracian; and a girl of whom a sculptor at Sicyon would have made two, was, according to their accepted measure, a wonder of a nymph. As Andromeda was to be very thinly clad, Eucolpis, who was well aware in what consisted the power of her charms, invented a drapery of pink muslin, under which very little of her beauty was lost to the spectators, while at the same time the proprieties were not altogether forgotten; under such circumstances, of what earthly consequence was it whether she sang well or ill? Had the music been if possible more tasteless, and her acting ten times more faulty, she would have been equally obliged to repeat her monologue, because it afforded the most respectable pretext for keeping her so long before the eager eyes of the spectators.

" This is indeed, by Jupiter! a splendid piece," said one to the other, with half-closed eyes— " an incomparable piece! Do you not think that Eucolpis sings like a goddess to-day? "

" Oh! beyond all expression—it is, by Anubis! just as if Euripides had written the drama on purpose for her." The young gentleman who thus spoke, used always to swear by Anubis, to show he had been in Egypt.

The ladies, as it is easy to guess, did not find the Andromeda so wonderful as their lords.

" Middling—pretty well," said they. " But how
does it happen that the characters have been
so unfortunately cast? The play loses by it—
the characters ought to have been changed
—and the stout Eucolpis should have taken
that of the mother! she would do very well for
a Cassiopeia." A great deal of criticism was
put forth about her hair, dress, &c.; she was
not at all attired to her advantage—the girdle
was placed too high, and drawn too tight, and
above all, her affectation in putting her feet forward was vexatious, she was evidently proud
of their disproportionate smallness." So said
the ladies, who for contrary reasons used to
conceal their own.

At the same time, both ladies and gentlemen
agreed that she sang delightfully—and that
nothing could excel the aria in which she
lamented her fate. Eucolpis, although her
acting was bad, possessed a very good, sonorous,
and melodious voice. But that which had
made her the favourite singer of Abdera, was,
that she endeavoured to imitate certain modulations of the nightingale, which pleased both
herself and the audience so much, that she
introduced them everywhere — at the wrong
time, as well as at the right: they were, notwith-

standing, always welcome. Whatever she might have to do—to laugh or to cry—to hope or to fear—to be angry or imploring—she always found occasion to introduce her nightingale notes, even though she spoiled the best passages by so doing.

As to the actors who personated Perseus, as the principal lover of Andromeda, Agenor her late lover, her father, her mother, and a priest of Neptune, we have nothing to say, except that many objections might be made to them in detail, although on the whole they satisfied their audience tolerably well. Perseus was a fine grown young man, and possessed great talent, as an Abderite Grimaldi, which was his proper character. The before-mentioned Cyclops, in the satirical play of that name, by Euripides, was his chief performance.

" He performed the Perseus very well," said the Abderite ladies; " but it was a pity that the Cyclops sometimes comes in unawares."

Cassiopeia, a pert, apish little creature, full of affected graces, had not one natural tone, but she stood high in the favour of the wife of the second archon, she possessed a very droll manner, had little songs to sing, and did the best she could.

The priest of Neptune roared a powerful sailor's bass—and Agenor sang miserably,
as it became a rejected lover to do—it is true he
sang no better when he had to play a first part,
but as he was a tolerable dancer, he had a sort of
privilege to sing the worse. " He dances beautifully," was always the answer of the Abderites,
when it was remarked that his croaking was
insupportable—in the meantime Agenor seldom
had to dance, although he sang in all the concerts and operas.

In order fully to understand the beauties of
the Andromeda, it is necessary to imagine two
choruses—one, of the Nereids, and the other
of the attendants of Andromeda ; both consisting
of disguised school-boys, who demeaned themselves so ridiculously, that, to the great comfort of
the Abderites, they had enough to laugh at, especially the chorus of the Nereids, owing to an
invention introduced by the nomophylax, which
had the most stupendous effect. The Nereides
appeared with the upper half of their persons
above water, with false golden hair and busts
as feminine as could be contrived. The sym-
phony to which these sea-wonders swam out,
was an imitation of the celebrated " Brekekek,
koax, koax," in the Frogs of Aristophanes, and

to make the illusion more perfect, Gryllus introduced cow-horns, which came on from time to time to imitate the Tritons blowing their sea-shells or conches.

For the sake of brevity, we will say nothing more about the decorations than that they were thought "very pretty" by the Abderites. A sunset in particular was admired, which was produced by a windmill, whose sails were furnished with long lighted matches. This, said they, "would have produced the most beautiful effect, had it been turned round a little quicker."

A connoisseur might also have wished that when Perseus flew up the stage in his winged sandals, the strings by which he was suspended, had been painted the colour of the atmosphere, so as not to come so distinctly before the eyes.

But on the whole the Andromeda was a "decided success."

CHAPTER VI.

As soon as the play was over, and the stunning applause a little relaxed, there was a general inquiry, as usual, of " Well, how do you like the drama?" followed of course with the usual answer.

One young gentleman, who passed for a perfect connoisseur, put the great question to a somewhat elderly stranger, sitting in one of the middle stalls, and who, from his appearance, seemed not to be an ordinary man. The foreigner, who had probably remarked that it was of very little use to answer except in one way, said, pretty readily, " Very much;" but as the tone made his approbation appear suspicious, and as it was accompanied by an almost imperceptible shrug of the shoulders, the young gentleman would not allow him to escape so cheaply, so he said—

" It seems the play does not please you. It is, however, known as one of the best of Euripides !"

" Indeed ! the piece is not so much amiss," replied the stranger.

" Then it is the music that you object to ?"

" Oh ! as to the music, it is such as can be heard only in Abdera."

" You are very kind ! In fact our nomophylax is very great in his art."

" Certainly."

" Then you are not satisfied with the performers ? "

" I am satisfied with everybody."

" I thought Andromeda played her part charmingly."

" Oh, yes, charmingly."

" She produces a great effect, does she not ?"

" You understand that best, I am not young enough."

" At least you will allow that Perseus is a great actor ? "

" Precisely so ; a very handsome, well-made, man."

" And the choruses ; these are choruses which

do honour to their master ! Do you not think the idea of introducing the Nereids in that manner a very happy one ?"

The stranger seemed to have had enough of the Abderite. "I think (he replied a little impatiently) that the Abderites are very fortunate in being so well satisfied with everything."

"Sir," said the young man, in a tone of irony, "rather confess that the play has not had the good fortune and honour to please you."

"Of what import to you is my approbation ? the majority decides."

"There you are right ; but I wish, for the wonder's sake, to hear what you could have to say against our actors and music."

"What I could," said the stranger, somewhat hastily; but he soon checked himself. "Excuse me, I will not dispute with any one concerning what gives him satisfaction. The play, as it is here performed, is universally liked in Abdera; what more can you desire ?"

"Not universally, it has not pleased you."

"I am a foreigner."

"But, foreigner or not, I should like to hear your reasons. Ha ! ha ! ha ! your reasons— your reasons, they won't be foreign I suppose."

The stranger began to lose his patience.

" Young gentleman, I have paid for my entertainment, and have applauded just as much as anybody else; there let it rest! I am going to continue my journey, I have business to attend to."

" Eh! Eh!" said another young Abderite who had listened to this conversation. " You will not leave us so soon, I hope; you seem to be a great connoisseur, you have excited our curiosity,— our desire to learn, (he said this with the jeering laugh of a conceited boy,) we cannot indeed let you go till you tell us what you see to censure in to-day's performance; I will not say anything about the text, I am no connoisseur in that, but the music, I dare to say, was incomparable."

" But after all, the text, as you call it, must decide that," said the stranger.

" What do you mean by that ? I think music is music, and only ears are necessary to hear what is pretty."

" I concede, if you wish it, that this music had some pretty passages, it may be scientific music, set according to all the rules of art— scholastic and artistic; I have nothing to say against it, except that it is not adapted to the Andromeda of Euripides!"

" You mean that the words ought to be better expressed ? "

" Oh ! the words are sometimes too well expressed ; but, on the whole, gentlemen, the intention of the author is lost sight of. The characters in the drama, the truth of the affections and impressions, the real appropriateness of the situation—all that music must be in order to become the language of nature—the language of passion ; all that enables the author to float over it as his native element, and be upborn, but not submerged ; all this has been completely mistaken or forgotten—in fact the whole is worth nothing—there ! you have my opinion in three words."

The vivacity with which both the defenders of their country's taste attacked the white-bearded stranger, attracted to them several other Abderites, all attentive to the dispute which seemed to bear so much upon the credit of the national stage. All pressed round him at once, and although a tall and stately man, he found it necessary to lean against a pillar, to protect at least his back. " How I prove that," replied he quietly ; " I shall not prove it at all ! What ! after having read the piece, seen the performance, and heard the music, you ask me for proofs of my opinion !—I should lose time and waste breath were I to talk further on the subject with you."

"The gentleman is not very easily satisfied, as I perceive," said a senator, who came forward to join in the conversation, and for whom both the young men respectfully made room. "We have all two ears in Abdera; liberty is left to everybody,—but still—"

"How! what! what is the matter!" cried the short stout senator, waddling up. "Has the gentleman anything to say against this piece? I should like to hear it—ha! ha! ha! one of the best pieces, upon my soul, which has for a long time been brought out. Much action! very much—a—a, what was I about to say? a beautiful play, and an admirable moral."

"Gentlemen," said the foreigner, "I came to Abdera on business, and looked into your theatre for a little recreation; I have applauded, according to the custom of your country, and would have gone quietly away, had not these young gentlemen compelled me, in the most peremptory manner, to give them my opinion."

"You have a perfect right so to do," replied the other senator, who secretly was not a great admirer of the nomophylax, and who, upon political grounds, had for some time been seeking an opportunity of getting rid of him in a courteous manner. "You are a connoisseur in music it seems."

"I speak according to my convictions," replied the stranger.

The Abderites around him became more and more clamorous. At last Gryllus himself, hearing that a discussion about the music was going forward, appeared on the spot. He had a very peculiar way of drawing his eyes together, turning up his nose, and shrugging his shoulders, when he intended to express contempt for a person with whom he found himself brought into collision.

"Well," he said, "my composition has not had the good fortune to please the gentleman; he is a connoisseur!—ha! ha! ha! he certainly understands music! yes."

"It is the nomophylax," whispered some one in the ear of the stranger, in order to bring him down at one blow, by discovering the high station of the man whose works he had judged so severely.

The stranger made his obeisance to the nomophylax, as was the custom in Abdera, and remained silent.

"Well, I should like to hear what the gentleman has to say against the composition! I do not answer for the faults of the orchestra, but a hundred drachmas for a fault in the composition—ha! ha! ha! well, let us hear."

"I do not know what you call faults," said the stranger. "In my opinion the music of which we are speaking has but one fault."

"And that is—" asked the nomophylax, elevating his nose.

"That the sense and the spirit of the author are entirely misrepresented," replied the foreigner.

"It is nothing more! then I did not understand the author, and you of course do—ha! ha! ha! Do you think we know nothing of Greek here? or perhaps you have entered into the head of the poet?—ha! ha! ha!"

"I know what I am talking about," replied the stranger, "and if it must be so, I beg leave to protest, verse after verse, through all the piece—and before all Greece."

"It would give you too much trouble," said the polite alderman.

"There is no occasion for it!" cried the nomophylax; "a vessel sails to-morrow for Athens, and I will write to Euripides—to the author, and send him the whole of the music!

This gentleman certainly does not pretend to understand the play better than its own author; all here bear witness that Euripides himself shall decide the question."

"You may spare yourself that trouble," said the stranger, smiling, "because, and to end at once this discussion, I am Euripides to whom you would appeal!"

Of all the unlucky tricks that Euripides could have played the nomophylax of Abdera, this was certainly the least endurable, to be there himself in person, just at the moment when he had threatened to appeal to him. But who could imagine such a thing! What, by Anubis! had he to do in Abdera? and just at the moment, too, when one would prefer seeing a wolf, to seeing him! Had he been in Athens as was believed, (and where he resided,) all would have proceeded in the usual way; the nomophylax would have accompanied his composition with a polite letter, and have added to his name all his titles and honours. This would have had its effect. Euripides would have sent back an equally polite.and Attic reply, Gryllus would have read it to all Abdera, and who could have then contested with him his victory over the foreigner! But that the stranger—

the clever, criticising stranger who told the nomophylax to his face what no one belonging to Abdera would have dared to have done, should prove to be Euripides himself,—this was one of those accidents for which a man like Gryllus could never have been prepared, and was sufficient to raise a blush in the face of any man but an Abderite.

The nomophylax generally contrived to extricate himself out of any difficulty, but nevertheless this blow first stunned him absolutely.

"Euripides!" he cried, and retreated three paces backward.

"Euripides!" reiterated at the same moment the politic senator, his short, stout colleague, both the young gentlemen and the whole circle of bystanders all looking around them as if to see from what cloud he had fallen.

A man is never less inclined to believe than when he is surprised by the fact which he had never considered as possible. This, then, was Euripides, the same of whom they had just spoken—the author of the Andromeda—to whom the nomophylax had threatened to write! was it possible?

The politic senator was the first to recover from the general consternation.

"A happy occurrence," said he, "by Castor! a happy circumstance.   Mr. Nomophylax! now you need not copy your music, and besides, you can spare yourself the trouble of writing your letter."

The nomophylax felt the incalculable importance of the moment, and if it be a mark of a great man to seize at a decisive juncture the only means of extricating himself from a difficulty, it must be confessed that Gryllus might claim to be recognized as such.

"Euripides!" he exclaimed. "What! has the gentleman become Euripides all of a sudden? Ha! ha! ha! the idea is excellent; but here, in Abdera, it is not easy to make people believe that black is white."

"It would be amusing," said the stranger, "if here, in Abdera, I should not be allowed the right to use my name!"

"I beg your pardon, sir," interrupted the sycophant of Thrasyllus, "not the right to your name, but the right to proclaim yourself the Euripides to whom the nomophylax threatened to appeal. You may bear the name of Euripides, but to be the author of the Andromeda is quite another question."

"Gentlemen, I will be anything you like, if

it please you to let me go. I promise you my first step will be the direct way to your town gate, and the nomophylax may put me in an opera if ever I come back again."

"No, no, no! we cannot part with him so quickly. The gentleman has represented himself as Euripides, and now that he sees the case is becoming serious he wants to retreat. No! we cannot consent to this; he must prove that he is Euripides, or, as sure as my name is Gryllus—"

"Do not put yourself in a passion, my friend," said the politic alderman; "it is true I am not a physiognomist, but the stranger, to my eyes, looks like Euripides, and I should advise you to pause—"

"I wonder," said one of the bystanders, "that so much time should be lost, when the whole affair could be settled by a 'no' or a 'yes.' There, across the park, stands a statue of Euripides; we have nothing more to do than to judge whether the stranger is like the statue."

"Bravo! bravo!" cried the short stout senator. "This is advice from a sensible man: ha! ha! ha! the statue must decide! there is no mistake about it!—the statue must decide, although it cannot speak!—ha! ha! ha!"

The bystanders laughed heartily at the witty idea of the fat little legislator, and all who were nimble enough ran to the park. The stranger surrendered himself to his fate with a good. grace, and allowed them to examine him before and behind, and compare him piece by piece with the statue, as long as they thought proper to do so;—but, alas! the comparison could not serve him, because the statue was no more like Euripides than any other man in particular.

"Well!" cried the nomophylax in triumph; "what can the gentleman say now in his defence?"

"I can say," replied the stranger, who seemed to enjoy the comedy, "what no one of you appears to be aware of,—although it is too true, that you are Abderites, and I am Euripides."

"You may say! you may say!" grinned the nomophylax;—"ha! ha! ha! and what *can* you say?"

"I say that the statue has not the slightest resemblance to Euripides."

"No, sir, you must not say so. The bust is a beautiful one; it is of white marble, as you may see, the marble of Paros, by Jove! and it cost us a hundred darics in ready money—you may believe me. It is the production of our city-sculptor, a clever and celebrated man : his name is Moschior—you have heard of him, I suppose? a celebrated man! and, as is well known, all strangers who have visited us have admired the bust : it is genuine, you may depend upon it! you can see your name (as you affirm it to be) is written underneath in gold letters—

ΕΥΡΙΠΙΔΗΣ.

" Gentlemen," said the stranger (who was obliged to use no small degree of self-control to prevent bursting with laughter), " may I put to you one question only ? "

" Most willingly," said the Abderites.

" Suppose there arises a contest between me and my bust which resembles me the most; which would you believe, me or the bust ? "

" That is a curious inquiry," said one of the Abderites, scratching his ear. " A captious question, by Jove !" cried another. "Be cautious what you do reply, worshipful Mr. Senator."

" Is the stout gentleman a senator of this celebrated republic ? " asked the stranger with a bow ; "then I beg your pardon. I allow that the bust is a nicely-polished work of beautiful Parian marble ; and if it does not resemble me, it arises only from the bust being made much better-looking by your celebrated sculptor than I am by nature—in any case, it is a proof of his good-will, and it deserves all my gratitude."

This compliment produced a great effect, as the Abderites were fond of being addressed in a courteous and polite manner. "It must, after all, be Euripides in person," they murmured one to the other; and even the stout senator remarked, after a slight comparison of the bust with the foreigner, that there seemed to be something of a likeness in the beard.

Fortunately, at this moment the archon Onolaus, with his nephew Onobalus, came up; the latter had seen Euripides a hundred times in Athens, and had often conversed with him. The joy of the young man at this unexpected meeting, and his positive affirmation that the stranger was really the celebrated Euripides, cut the knot at once, and the majority of the Abderites assured each other that they had perceived it at the first glance.

The nomophylax, seeing that Euripides had gained his cause against the bust, made off grumbling—"A vile trick," he muttered. "Why was he so reserved! knowing that he was Euripides, why did he not introduce himself to me!

Things would then have taken quite a different turn !"

The archon, who used always in such cases to do the honours of the city of Abdera, invited the author, with great politeness, to accept his hospitality: he also invited both the senators present to favour him with their company for the evening, which invitation they accepted with great pleasure.

"Did I not say at once," said the stout legislator to one who was standing near, "that it was Euripides in person? The beard, the nose, the forehead, the shape of the ear, the eyes, all to a hair! I never saw anything so like! where was the perception of the nomophylax! But— yes, yes, yes, he had taken a little,—hem!—you understand me! '*Cantores amant humores,*' ha! ha! ha! But enough, we have Euripides amongst us! a fine man, by Jove! and one who will make us a great deal of fun! ha! ha! ha!"

CHAPTER VII.

How Euripides came to be in Abdera, and some secret
notices concerning the court at Pella.

However possible it was that Euripides should
be in Abdera just at the moment when the nomophylax least expected or wished for him, and
however accustomed we are to such unexpected
apparitions on the stage, it becomes a very different matter when they take place in the pit of the
theatre, so, by the majesty of history, we are bound
to make the reader understand how it happened,
and to relate faithfully all we know about it.

Well, all we know about it is this. The king,
Archelaus of Macedon, a great lover of the
fine arts and of fine minds,* conceived the idea
of having his own court theatre, and from a
concatenation of circumstances, reasons, inten-

* A phrase applied to the spoiled children of nature,
and which we use when we hardly know in what other
terms to describe them.

tions, and aims, which cannot interest anybody
in our days, he succeeded in engaging Euripides on very advantageous terms to come to
Pella with a troop of chosen actors, virtuosi,
builders, painters, and machinists—in short, with
all that was requisite—to take the direction of
this court theatre.

It was on this journey that Euripides was proceeding with his company, and notwithstanding
that the best and shortest road did not lead
through Abdera, he preferred this route, having
a great desire to see a republic so famous for the
wit of its inhabitants. How it happened that he
arrived just on the day that the Andromeda of
the nomophylax was performed, we cannot say;
but similar *apropos* occur more frequently than
is believed, and are no greater wonders than
other occurrences. For the rest, if we say that
King Archelaus was a great *amateur* of the fine
arts, it must not be taken too strictly, or in the
strongest sense of the words, because it, is after
all, only a figure of speech : in fact, this king was
not much of a connoisseur. The truth was, His
Majesty was often troubled with *ennui*, all his
former amusements having become wearisome
from their repetition. Besides, he was a man of
great ambition, and had been told by his cham-

berlain that it was necessary for a great ruler to protect and encourage the arts and sciences— "Because," said the chamberlain, "your Majesty must have remarked that no statue, or bust, or medal of a great potentate can be seen without a Minerva standing on his right hand, and close by a trophy of armour, standards, lances, and maces; on the left are always kneeling some winged youths, or half-naked girls, with pencils and palettes, a parallel ruler, a flute, a lyre, and a roll of paper in their hands, representing the arts, who seem to be asking his protection; over all these flies Fame, with a trumpet in her mouth, to show that kings and princes gain immortal glory by becoming the protectors of the arts," &c.

So King Archelaus took the arts under his protection, and accordingly the historians have given us long and pompous descriptions of all he built; of how much he spent in paintings and statues, rich carpets, and elegant furniture; and how everything was to be "Etruscan" with him, even down to his stew-pans; and how he invited to his court celebrated artists, virtuosi, and others: all this, say they, he did to efface the crimes by which he raised himself to a throne which he was not born to inherit, as may, with much more to the same purpose, be seen in Bayle and elsewhere.

After this little digression, return we to our Attic author, whom we shall meet in a brilliant circle of Abderite ladies and gentlemen, all "*créme de la créme*," sitting under a green pavilion in the garden of the archon Onolaus.

CHAPTER VIII.

How Euripides behaved himself among the Abderites.—
They devise a plot against him, from which will be
seen their polite activity, and which is the more sure
to succeed, as all the difficulties they see in it are
only imaginary ones.

It has been remarked in a preceding chapter
that Euripides, although personally unknown to
them, had long been held in high consideration
by the Abderites. Now, as soon as it was
known that he was present in person, the whole
town was in a ferment. Nothing was talked of
but Euripides.

"Have you seen Euripides?"

"How does he look?"

"Has he a large nose?"

"How does he hold his head?"

"What sort of eyes has he?"

"Of course he speaks only in verse?"

" Is he proud?"

And a hundred such questions, which were asked quicker than one could be answered.

The anxiety to see Euripides brought together many more than those who had been invited by the archon. All pressed around the good bald-pated author, to see if he looked as they had imagined ; many, especially among the ladies, seemed to wonder that after all he looked so much like other people !   Others remarked that he seemed to have a great deal of fire in his eyes, and the pretty Thrysallis whispered in the ear of her neighbour that he appeared a determined woman-hater.*   She made this remark with an expression of pleasure at the triumph she anticipated, hoping that the power of her charms would make an impression on such an enemy of her sex.

Stupidity has its sublime as well as genius, and he who carries that quality to absurdity has reached it, which is always a source of pleasure to sensible people.   The Abderites had the good fortune to have attained to this degree of perfection.   Their unreasonableness at first sometimes

* It is well known that Euripides was accused of this terrible defect, although without deserving it.

made a foreigner impatient, but as soon as it was clear that they were all of a piece and had a great deal of trust in others, and equal confidence in themselves, it was easy to be reconciled to them, and in fact to derive more pleasure from their absurdities than from the wit of other people.

Euripides was never in so good a humour as with the Abderite party. He answered all their questions with the greatest politeness; laughed at all their silly conceits; let every one be valued according to his own valuation; and expressed himself concerning their theatre and music so agreeably, that everybody was satisfied.

"An exalted intellect!" said the politic senator to the Lady Salabanda, who was seated near him.

"That is easily seen—and so polite, and as modest as if he were not a great man!" replied Salabanda.

"The most amusing man in the world, by Jove!" said the short, stout legislator, on rising from table; "a very amusing man! I should not have supposed it, upon my soul!"

The ladies, whom he was wise enough to think very pretty, were well pleased, and treated him as if he had been twenty years younger than he was. In short, every one was enchanted with him, and only regretted that they could not have the pleasure and the honour of entertaining him longer in Abdera, because Euripides insisted that he must take his departure immediately.

At last the Lady Salabanda took the politic senator and the young Onobulus aside. "What would you say if we could induce him to give us his Andromeda? He has his own company with him; they must be extraordinary artists."

Onobulus thought the idea sublime. "I had the same thought just now," said the senator, "and was about to communicate it to you; but there are difficulties—the nomophylax?"

"Oh, for that, leave it to me," replied Salabanda; "I will make him warmly espouse the project."

"I will answer for my uncle," said Onobulus; "and this very night I will collect a party amongst our young men, who will strenuously support it in the city."

"Be not so rash," answered the serious senator, shaking his head; "we must not yet make ourselves so conspicuous. First the ground must be tried, and we must proceed gradually. This was always my doctrine."

"But we have no time to lose, Mr. Frog-keeper: * Euripides is going away."

"We will keep him longer," said Salabanda. "He is coming to me to-morrow; a garden-party and all the *élite* are invited. Leave it to me; the thing is certain."

Lady Salabanda passed in Abdera for a very clever person. She was a strong politician, and had great influence over the archon Onolaus. The high-priest was her uncle, and five or six senators, whom she counted in her friendly circle, seldom gave any other opinion in the sittings than what she had arranged for them on the previous evening.

Besides these, the admirers of the lovely Thrysallis, with whom she lived in the greatest intimacy, were at her command, without mentioning her own, who lived upon hope, and were consequently as pliant as gloves. Her house, which was one of the first in the town, was the place where all business was prepared before-hand, all disputes finished, and where all elections were brought to a final decision. In one

---

* The senator was one of the guardians of the holy frog-pool, which in Abdera was considered a very high post. They were called *batrachotrophists*, which may be very properly expressed in English as frog-keepers.

word, the Lady Salabanda could do in Abdera whatever she wished.

Euripides, without the least intention of making use of the influence of this lady, had insinuated himself into her favour as much as if he had been desirous of an appointment as frog-keeper. If she introduced common-place notions on a political topic, he observed what a very sagacious remark it was! Did she quote Simonides, or Homer, he admired her talent for declamation. She had rallied him about some passages in his works which had gained him in Athens the bad reputation of being an enemy to the fair sex, and he assured her and the pretty Thrysallis, bowing to them, that his disgrace was the consequence of his not having come before to Abdera. In short, he behaved so well that Lady Salabanda was prepared to encourage a revolution, if she could not succeed by milder means in executing the project she had plotted with the politic senator. They took care, without delay, to secure the archon, who was generally very easily persuaded if he was assured that anything would tend to the glory of the republic and the gratification of the people; but, as he was a gentleman very solicitous about his own peace and quiet, he declared that he left it

to them to arrange everything in a proper way—
for himself, he should not like to come into
collision with anybody, and least of all with
the nomophylax, who was an impertinent fellow,
but very popular among the people.

"As to the people, I would say, do not let your
excellency take any trouble," whispered the senator to him; "I shall transact it all by a third
party, and without your appearing in the matter."

"And I will take the senate upon myself,"
said Salabanda.

"We shall see!" said the archon, returning
to the company.

"Be quiet!" said the lady to her senatorial
friend, stepping aside with him. "I know
the archon; if you wish to have him with you,
he must be spoken to about the matter only
once in the evening, and if he says 'No,' you
must come the next morning without any
concern, and speak to him as if he had said
'Yes;' showing at the same time what you
are sure would be the result. In this way you
may depend on him as on gold. It is not
the first time that I have caught him in this
manner."

"You are a clever woman!" replied Mr.
Frog-keeper, tapping her gently on her rounded

arm; "only you are going too fast! But they perceive we are discussing something, and the effect may not be good; let us speak in a lower tone."

At that moment the Abderite ladies tripped up to them, followed by the rest of the company, to learn what they were talking about. The senator slipped away.

" Well, how are you pleased with Euripides ? " said Salabanda; " he is a dear man, is he not ? "

"Oh, a charming man!" cried all the fair Abderites.

" Pity only that he is bald ! " added another.

" And that two of his teeth are gone ! " said a third.

" You little simpleton ! he is less able to bite you ! " replied a fourth; and as this was considered a witty conceit, they all laughed heartily.

"Is he married?" asked a young thing who looked like a mushroom sprung up during the night.

" You would like perhaps to have him ? " replied another young lady, satirically; " I think he has grandchildren to marry ! "

" Oh, I would leave them for you ! " said the younger one, tartly; and this stab was the keener, as the said young lady, though dressed like a girl of eighteen, had her forty-fifth year on her shoulders.

"Children!" interrupted Salabanda, "talk no more of these things; something else is on the carpet. What would you say if I could persuade the stranger to stay here some days, and give us one of his plays by his own company of actors?"

"Oh, delightful!" exclaimed all the Abderite ladies, anxious for pleasure; "oh yes! could you do it?"

"I am willing to do it," replied Salabanda, "but you must assist me."

"Oh yes! oh yes!" cried all the ladies, and then they ran in a crowd to Euripides, and all cried out at once, "Mr. Euripides, you must perform a play for us! We will not let you depart till you have given us a play! Will you? you promise it?"

The poor man, on whose head this proposal came like an unexpected shower-bath, stepped back, and assured them that he never thought of performing a play in Abdera, he must proceed at once upon his journey, &c.; but all this availed him nought.

"We will not let you have any rest, and we are sure you are too kind to refuse; we will ask you so sweetly."

"In fact," said Salabanda, "we have formed a decided plot against you."

"And one which shall not fail, or my name is not Onobulus!" interrupted the young man.

"What is the matter? What is going forward now?" said the senator, who feigned ignorance, and approached slowly, with an uncertain glance; "what are you about with the gentleman?"

His fat colleague came waddling up also,— "I believe, the Gods bless me! that you will take his heart into custody—he! he! he!" and he laughed so that he was obliged to hold his sides.

They enlightened him about the matter.

"Ha! ha! ha! a pretty conceit, bless me, Jupiter! I join in it, I promise you. The author himself! That will be worth seeing; it will confer great honour on Abdera—a great honour, friend Euripides. It will rejoice us to see our people profiting by so excellent a master."

Several other gentlemen of consequence expressed themselves nearly in the same way.

Euripides, who, in fact, did not think the idea a bad one, as it would give him a great deal of amusement with the Abderites, still affected astonishment, and excused himself by saying that he had promised King Archelaus to make haste on his journey.

"Eh! what?" said Onobulus; "you are a republican, so a republic has a greater claim upon you than a king."

"Only tell His Majesty," said the beautiful Myris, "that we asked you so prettily! He is a courteous gentleman, and will not blame you because you could not refuse a request preferred by six ladies at once."

"Oh Love! great king of Gods and men!" exclaimed Euripides in a tragic tone, looking at the same time at the pretty Thrysallis.

"If you are serious," said Thrysallis, with the accent of a person who is not accustomed either to refuse or be refused; "if you are in earnest, prove it by yielding to my wishes."

This "my wishes" very much vexed the other fair Abderites.

"We must not be importunate," said one of them aside.

"We must not ask the gentleman anything that it is impossible for him to do," said another.

"To give you pleasure, lovely ladies," said the poet, "the impossible would become possible to me."

As this was nonsense it pleased every one. Onobulus took out his tablets, and hastily wrote down the words with his stylet. The women and girls cast a look at Thrysallis, as much as to say, " See, he called us lovely too ! There is no occasion for madam to be so proud of her face; he remains here not only for her, but for us."

Salabanda finally put an end to the confusion by asking of him only the kindness to grant her and her friends, who were all his warm admirers, but one day more. Euripides, who, in fact, found himself amused in Abdera, and in no hurry to leave, did not require repeated solicitations from the ladies, so he accepted an invitation which would afford him materials for a farce at the court of Pella.

The company therefore agreed to meet next day at Salabanda's, and separated with much pleasure at midnight.

CHAPTER IX.

Euripides inspects the town.—Makes the acquaintance
of the priest Strobylus, and hears from him the history
of Latona's frogs.—Remarkable conversation between
Democritus, the priest, and the poet.

In the mean time, Onobulus, in company with
several young gentlemen of his grade, conducted
their guest the next day over the town, to show
him all that was remarkable in it.

On the way they were met by Democritus,
who had long before been acquainted with the
author.   They walked together, and as the town
was extensive, the elder gentlemen had every
opportunity of profiting by the information of
the younger ones (whose mouths were always
open).   They knew everything, decided on
everything, and it never occurred to them that
it might have been more becoming to listen, in
the society of such men, than to expect to be
listened to.

Euripides had enough to hear and see that morning. The young Abderites, who had never been beyond the gates of their native town, spoke of everything which they pointed out as of wonders which had no equal in the world. Onobulus, on the contrary, who had made "the great tour," compared everything he had seen of the same kind at Athens, Corinth, Syracuse, and found stupid apologies for the admitted fact that they were more striking and magnificent in those cities than in Abdera.

"Young man," said Democritus, "it is right that you should honour all that belongs to your native city; but if you wish to give us a proof of it, set aside Athens, Corinth, and Syracuse. Let us take everything as it is, and no comparisons; then we shall want no excuses."

Euripides found everything that was pointed out to him "wonderful." A library was shown to him, containing a great number of useless and unread books, and a collection of coins, many of which were only imitations; a rich hospital with many poor patients badly attended; an arsenal with but few weapons, and a fountain with still less water. The town-hall was pointed out to him, where the good town of Abdera was so well regulated, and the temple of Jason with the gilded ram's-skin, which they represented as the celebrated golden fleece, although very little gold could now be seen upon it. They viewed the old smoky temple of Latona, and the tomb of Abderus, who founded the city, and the gallery where all the archons of Abdera were represented the size of life, and looked as like each other as if each succeeding one was a copy of the former. Finally, when they had seen everything else, they were conducted to the sacred pool, where croaked the largest and fattest frogs that were ever seen, fed at the common expense of the town, and which, as the priest Strobylus seriously assured them, derived their descent from the Lycian peasants, who refused to allow the weary and thirsty Latona to drink from their ditch, for which they had been condemned by Jupiter to be transformed into frogs.

"Reverend sir," said Democritus, " do tell the foreign gentleman the story of these frogs, and how it occurred that the sacred ditch of Lycia came over the Ionian sea, which, as you know, is at a great distance from Abdera—over mountains and deserts—and which, I may say, is a greater miracle than even the transformation of the Lycian peasants into frogs."

Strobylus cast a sharp glance at the eyes of the stranger and Democritus ; but as he did not discover anything there to indicate that they were scoffers who did not deserve to be initiated in such high mysteries, he asked them to sit down under a large fig-tree which overshadowed one side of Latona's little temple, and related to them all he knew about the matter, with as much simplicity as if it were an every-day occurrence.

"The story of the worship of Latona in Abdera," said he, "is lost in the mist of remotest antiquity. Our ancestors, the Teïans, who became masters of Abdera 140 years ago, found that it had been established from a most distant period, and the temple is perhaps the oldest in the world, as you may judge from its construction and other visible signs of antiquity. It is not allowed, as you know, to raise with censurable zeal the sacred veil thrown over the origin of deities and their worship. All is lost in the times previous to the art of writing. But verbal traditions from father to son are, as far as may be necessary, a substitute for written chronicles, and are, so to speak, a living chronicle even preferable to dead letters. This tradition says, that at the time of the transformation of the

Lycian peasants, the inhabitants of the neighbourhood, and those peasants who did not share in
the crime, recognized (as witnesses of the miracle)
Latona, with her twins Apollo and Diana at her
breast, as deities ; built, on the spot where the
transformation took place, an altar; and proclaimed
the wooded country around the ditch as a sacred
grove. The country was then called Milia, or
Milias, and the peasants transformed were properly spoken of as Milians; but a long time afterwards Lycus, the second son of Pandion, with an
Attic colony, seized upon the country and gave
it the name of Lycia. On this occasion such
of the inhabitants as were unwilling to accept
the government of the said Lycus, left their
fatherland, embarked in many vessels, were
beaten about some time in the Ægæan Sea, and
finally settled in Abdera, which shortly before
had been entirely depopulated by a pestilence.
On their departure, nothing was so painful to
them as leaving the sacred pool of Latona.
After long reflection, they at last decided on
removing with them some young trees from
the holy grove, with their roots and the earth
about them, as well as a certain number of frogs
from the pool, in a cask filled with the sacred
water. On arriving at Abdera, their first con-

cern was to dig another pool, which is the very one you now see before you. They led an arm of the river Nestus into it, and filled it with the descendants of the Lycians or Milians transformed into the frogs, which they brought with them in the sacred water. They planted around the pool (to which they gave carefully the size and form of the old one) the young trees they brought with them, dedicated it again as Latona's grove, built this temple to her, and ordained a priest whose duty it is to perform the rites of her worship and watch over the grove and the stream, thus transplanted hither from Lycia, without that great miracle which Democritus imagines.

"This temple, as well as the grove and the pool, remained protected by the reverence which was paid to divine things, even by the wild Thracians, through all the changes and misfortunes to which Abdera had been subjected, till the city was rebuilt by our ancestors the Teïans, in the time of the great Cyrus, and reached, as may be said without vain-glory, that splendour which leaves us nothing to envy in any city in the world."

"You are speaking like a true patriot, vene-

rable high-priest," said Euripides. "But may
I ask you a modest question?"

"If you please—all that you wish," interrupted Strobylus. "I shall never be at a loss,
thank the gods! to give you an answer."

"Then, with your reverence's leave," proceeded Euripides, "all the world knows the
noble way of thinking, the love of splendour
and of the fine arts, which belongs to the Teïan
Abderites, and of which your town affords
everywhere the most striking proofs. How is
it, then, that as the Teïans have been known
from the remotest period as the worshippers
of Latona, the Abderites have never had the
idea of building for her a more magnificent
temple?"

"I expected this reproach," said Strobylus,
with a smile, elevating his eyes, and looking
wonderfully sagacious.

"It is not a reproach, but a simple question,"
replied Euripides.

"I will answer it," said the priest. "It
would doubtless have been easy for the republic
to have built a temple to Latona, suitable to a
goddess of the first class, since they erected so
magnificent a one to Jason, who was only a

hero, but the republic rightly understood that it was more in accordance with the respect we owe to the mother of Apollo and Diana to leave the ancient temple as we found it; and it is, and will continue to be, the principal and most sacred one in Abdera, notwithstanding anything that may be said against it by the priest of Jason."

Strobylus pronounced these words with so much vehemence, that Democritus thought it necessary to assure him that this would certainly be admitted by all right-thinking and well-informed people.

"In the mean time," continued the high-priest, "the republic has given such [proofs of its special devotion to the temple of Latona, and its accessories, that no doubt can be left about the purity of its intentions. They have appointed not only a college of ten priests for the service of her temple, of which college I have the honour of being the unworthy chief, but also, by the care of the senate, three guardians of the sacred pool are elected, the first of whom is always one of the heads of the State. The Government has also, from motives the rectitude of which we are not allowed to question, extended the inviolability of Latona's

frogs to all animals of this sort throughout
their territory, and for this reason have all the
storks, cranes, and other enemies of the frogs
been banished from Abdera."

"If the assurance that we are not allowed to
deny the rectitude of the proceeding had not
withheld me," said Democritus, "I might have
taken the liberty of suggesting to you that it
was established rather through a scruple or
superstition,* in itself laudable, but carried to
an unwarrantable extreme, rather than on the
nature of the thing, or from the reverence due
to Latona; because, in fact, nothing can be
more certain than that the frogs in Abdera and
the country around are already so troublesome
to the inhabitants, and will soon multiply to
such an extent through this protection, that I
cannot conceive how our descendants will be

* The apostle Paul makes use of this word in speaking ironically, or at least equivocally, of the unbounded
devotion of the Athenians. *Apost. Hist.* xvii. 22.   It
could be translated reverence for gods or demons.*—
Note by the Author.   [There appears no reason to suspect the apostle of any irony in the use of this expression.   The Athenians understood the word precisely in
the sense in which he employed it, and were evidently not
disposed to be otherwise than pleased with its application.—TRANSLATOR.]

able to tolerate them. I speak now only from a human point of view, and submit my opinion to the correction of my superior, as is becoming to a right-minded Abderite."

"In which you do well," said Strobylus, "whether you are in earnest or not; and would do still better (do not take it ill my suggesting as much to you) if you would not make such opinions known. After all, nothing can be more ridiculous than to live in fear of frogs, and I think, under the protection of Latona, we can afford to despise more dangerous foes than these good and innocent creatures—if, indeed, foes they should ever become."

"That is exactly my opinion," said Euripides, "and I wonder that so great a naturalist as Democritus does not see that the frogs, which live upon insects and young snakes, are rather useful than injurious to man."

The priest was so well pleased with this remark, that from that moment he became one of the greatest admirers and patrons of our poet.

Scarcely had the gentlemen taken leave, when he went into several of the principal houses, assuring every one that Euripides was a man of great merit. "I have remarked,"

said he, "that his opinions do not agree at
all with those of Democritus; he gave him more
than once a good rap over the knuckles.   He
is really a man of a very pretty understanding
—for a poet."

CHAPTER X.

AFTER Euripides had seen all the curiosities of
Abdera, he was conducted to the garden of
Salabanda, where he found her husband (a man
conspicuous only through his wife), and a large
circle of the Abderite *beau monde*, all very
anxious to learn what was to be done to become
a Euripides.

Euripides saw but one way of coming out
of the business with honour, and that was, to
be, in such goodly company, not Euripides, but,
as far as he possibly could, an Abderite. The
good people wondered to find him so like themselves.

"He is a charming man," they said; "it might be imagined that he had spent his life in Abdera."

The plot of Madame Salabanda went gallantly on, and the next morning all the town was full of the news that the foreign author was going to represent with his company a play the like of which was never before seen in Abdera.

It was the day the council sat; the learned gentlemen assembled, and asked each other when the play of Euripides was to be acted? Nobody chose to know anything about the matter, although all positively asserted that the preparations were in progress.

When the archon moved the business, many of the friends of the nomophylax were very much offended. "Why," said they, "is our permission to be asked, when the thing is already decided, and is spoken of by everybody as a certainty?"

One of the boldest contended, that for this very reason the senate ought to say "No," and show who were the masters.

"That would be a pretty business," said the guildmaster Awl. "Because the town is excited by the prospect and wishes to hear the foreign actors, the senate is to say '*no!*' I

support just the contrary : because the people
wish it, they ought to perform. '*Fox pobulus
fox Deus*'—this was always my ultimatum, and
shall remain so as long as I remain myself
head of the guild of cordwainers."

The greater part sided with Mr. Awl. The
politic senator shrugged his shoulders, spoke
for and against it, and concluded finally, " If
the nomophylax has nothing to say against it,
it might be left as tacitly understood, that
the foreigners should perform on the republican
stage."

Till this moment the nomophylax had only
turned up his nose, growled, stroked his whiskers,
and murmured a few broken words, interrupted
by a derisive " ha ! ha ! ha ! " He did not wish
to be thought very anxious to oppose the thing,
but the more he tried to conceal his opposition,
the more perceptible it was. He swelled like a
turkey-cock before which a red handkerchief is
held, and at last, as he had no choice but to
burst or to speak, he said,—

" Gentlemen may think whatever they like,
but I am really the most desirous among you to
hear the new piece. Undoubtedly the poet has
adapted the music to the words, and it will be
a real novelty. In the mean time, as his stay

must be so short, I do not see how the scenery can be ready; and if we are to have our people for the choruses, I am sorry to be obliged to say that there is no possibility of its coming off within a fortnight."

"That will be the business of Euripides himself!" said one of the senators, who was the mouthpiece of Salabanda; "and besides, we ought to leave to him the direction of his play."

"Without prejudice to the rights of the existing nomophylax, and the dramatic board," added the archon.

"I am satisfied with everything," said Gryllus. "The gentlemen wished for something new—well, I hope it will succeed! I am myself anxious to hear it. The only question here is, have we confidence in the people?—you understand me. In the mean time right will remain right, and music music; and I wager you all what you like, that the quavers, crotchets, and minims of the Athenians will sound exactly like ours. He! he! he!"

It was carried by a great majority, "That it shall be granted to the foreign comedians, *semel pro semper et citra consequentiam*, to perform a tragedy on the national stage, that every assistance shall be given them by the dramatic board, and that the expenses shall be paid from the theatrical fund."

But as the expression of "granted" might be displeasing to Euripides, who had asked nothing, Salabanda arranged that the reporter, who was her intimate friend and humble servant, should so far alter the decree as to change "*granted*" into "*requested*," and "*foreign comedians*" into "*the celebrated Euripides;*"—all this without prejudice to the rights of the senate and the board, and *citra consequentiam.*

As soon as the sitting was over, the nomo-phylax went to Euripides, overwhelmed him with compliments, offered his services, and assured him that every assistance should be afforded him to perform his piece as soon as possible. The result of this assurance was, that every impediment was thrown in his way (the blame of which could be thrown on no one), and that everything was deficient which was necessary. If he complained, one sent him to another, and they every one attested his inno-cence and good-will, making it distinctly to be understood that the fault rested on one or the other, who a quarter of an hour before had declared himself the most zealous in the service.

Euripides found the Abderite manner of

assistance so troublesome that he could not help declaring to Lady Salabanda, on the morning of the third day, his determination to profit by the first wind, from whatever quarter it might blow, to embark, as, contrary to the orders of the senate, the board gave him no assistance at all. As the archon, in whom all the executive power lay, was not a man of action, the only thing to be done in this difficulty was to set in motion the guildmaster Awl, and the priest Strobylus, who had great credit with the people.

Salabanda managed them both with such good effect, that in the space of four-and-twenty hours all was ready that was to have been done by the dramatic board, and which could be done so much easier, as Euripides had with him his own decorations, and they had nothing more to do than to adapt them to the Abderite theatre.

CHAPTER XI.

THE Abderites were expecting a new play, and consequently were dissatisfied that it was the Andromeda, which they fancied they had seen but a few days before. Still less could they approve of the foreign actors, whose tone and manner were so natural that the good people, who were accustomed to see heroes and heroines raving like mad people and crying out like the wounded Mars in the Iliad, could not comprehend what it meant.

"It is a strange kind of acting," whispered they to each other; "one cannot imagine one's self at the play : it sounds as if they were each performing their own individual character."

In the mean time they made known their admiration of the decorations, which were painted in theatrical perspective by a celebrated artist of Athens ; and as most of them had never seen anything really good of the kind, they were so bewitched with the representation of the sea-shore, and the rock to which Andromeda was chained, and the bower of the Nereids, with a little stream at one side, and the palace of King Cepheus on the other, that they could have sworn all was real and true as represented. Besides, the music was according to the idea of the poet, — was exactly what that of Gryllus was not, and consequently touched the heart ; notwithstanding its great simplicity, its melody was always new and surprising. All this, together with the great vivacity of the declamation and action, with the beauty of the voices and elocution, produced in the Abderites a sort of illusion which they had never experienced before.

They forgot that they were sitting in their national theatre, and imagined themselves in the real place of action, taking part in the good or bad fortune of the actors as if they were their nearest relations, and they were afflicted and uneasy, hoped and feared, loved and hated, wept or laughed, as it pleased the wizard in whose power they were. In short, the Andromeda impressed them so much, that Euripides himself avowed he had never before seen his play produce so much sensation.

We beg pardon (by way of parenthesis) of our young readers, especially those of the fairer sex, who, by dint of extreme sentiment, have arrived at last at the point of having no sentiment at all. It was not our intention to offend them by this description of the extraordinary simplicity of the Abderites, and, so to speak, to throw out seriously any imputation against themselves: we relate the thing as it occurred, and if this great sensibility of the Abderites appears so strange, we request them kindly to reflect, that, with all their Abderitism, they were men notwithstanding, and in a certain sense the more so because they were Abderites. They were as easily cheated as the birds which came to peck at the grapes painted by Zeuxis; they allowed themselves with the more innocence and sincerity to be led away by every impression, especially the illusions of art,—more easily, in fact, than finer and colder and consequently wiser men are accustomed to be.

Moreover, the author of this history observes, that the great disposition the Abderites had to be impressed by the arts of imagination and imitation, is not precisely what he liked the least in them. But for this he might have his particular reasons.

In fact, authors, musicians, and painters, have a very difficult game to play before a scientific and refined public; and the conceited connoisseurs who compose a great part of such public, are the most difficult to satisfy: instead of receiving impressions quietly, they do all they can to hinder them—instead of enjoying what is within reach, they are reasoning about what more is required—instead of giving way to an illusion where the destruction of the charm can only rob us of a pleasure, they make it a point of honour, I do not know why, to act the philosopher out of season; they force themselves to laugh when people with their natural feelings about them would have tears in their eyes; and where others would laugh, they turn up their noses, and give themselves airs of being too strong-minded, or too refined, to be moved by anything.

But even really sensible people spoil the enjoyment which they would derive from a thousand things good of their kind, by comparisons which are mostly unjust and always against their own interest, because what our pride gains by despising a pleasure is only a shadow at which we are grasping while the substance flies away.

At the same time it is clear that the poet must do his part in order to create and keep up the illusion; otherwise he has clearly no right to expect us, merely to please him, to act as though we saw what he does not show us, and felt what he does not impress on us.

We find, too, that it was exactly among the most barbarous races that the son of the music-god performed those wonders which men describe even yet, without exactly knowing what they are talking about. The woods in Thrace danced to the lyre of Orpheus, and the wild beasts crouched down at his feet, not because he was a demi-god, but because the Thracians were—wild beasts; not because he sang with superhuman melody, but because his hearers were unsophisticated children of nature;—in short, just for the same reason as, according to Forster's narrative, the good people of Tahiti fell into a frenzy of enthusiasm at the tones of a Scotch bagpipe.

The application of this not very new, but certainly very practical observation—an observation which everybody has heard often and often, but very few have thought worthy of attention—the reader may make for himself, if he feels inclined. Our own consciences may tell us how far we in other matters are Thracians or Abderites; but if we are in this particular, why—so much the better for us, and certainly for the greater number of our poetical bagpipers too.

CHAPTER XII.

How Abdera became mad with admiration of the Andromeda of Euripides.—Essay, philosophical and critical, upon the singular frenzy which is generally called by the old writers the Abderite epidemic.

WHEN the curtain fell, the Abderites still continued to look towards the stage with open eyes and mouths; and so great was their ecstasy, that they not only forgot their usual question, " How did you like the play?" but would have forgotten the clapping also, had not Salabanda and Onolaus, who first recovered themselves, broken the silence, and thus saved their fellow-citizens from the reproach of not having applauded on the first occasion that they would have been justified in doing so.

However, they made up, with interest, what had been so long neglected, and the clapping was no sooner commenced than it became most vehement and prolonged; those who were first exhausted recommencing after an interval with greater energy, till they were again relieved by those who had rested. But this was not sufficient; the good Abderites were so full of what they had heard and seen, that they were obliged to give vent to their feelings after another manner. Many of them stopped on their way home, in the public streets, repeating aloud such passages as had pleased them most, and with some the frenzy went so far as to impel them to sing, well or ill, as the case might be, what they retained in their memory of the exquisite music. Imperceptibly, the paroxysms (as is always the case) became general. A fairy seemed to have stretched her wand over Abdera, and changed all her inhabitants into so many comedians and singers. All who could breathe, spoke, sang, hummed, played, or whistled, sleeping and waking, day after day, passages from the Andromeda. Everywhere was heard the great solo,

"O Love! great king of gods and men," &c., &c.,

and it was sung so long, with variations, that at last nothing remained of the original melody, and finally it descended to the street-boys, who roared and whistled it through the streets all day.

If my advice had not the only fault of being impracticable, like that of many other wise men, I should hasten to recommend my readers never to believe anything that they hear, because the experience of thirty years has convinced me that no two relations of the same tale agree, and even an occurrence of yesterday, or of an hour ago, would not be related by two persons in the same manner; consequently there must always be some falsehood, as truth is ever consistent.

If this be the case with occurrences of our own time, in the place where we reside, and almost under our eyes, it is easy to see how far the historical truth of events that occurred long since may be depended on, for which we have only the warranty of written or printed books. Heaven knows how poor, respectable truth is cheated, and how much remains of her after having been, for one or two thousand years, sifted, drawn out, and compressed, by the medium of so many false traditions, chronicles, journals, pragmatical histories, abbreviated re-capitulations, historical dictionaries, collections of anecdotes, &c.; and after having passed through so many washed and unwashed hands of writers, copyists, compositors, translators,

censors, and correctors! For my part, I have
decided, from the observation of these things,
never to write the history of persons about
whose existence, or of events about whose
credibility, anybody cares!

I have been led to this digression by the
event before us, which has been so singularly
treated, and mal-treated, by different authors,
that the candid reader can scarcely form any
idea of it.

For instance, there is Yorick, the discoverer,
father, protoplast, and prototype of all sentimental journeys and sentimental travellers, who,
without purse or scrip, without having worn
out a single pair of shoes, travels for no other
object than to pay his beer and tobacco bills,—
I repeat, there is this Yorick, who, in order to
make an attractive chapter in his "Sentimental
Journey," dresses up this same story in such a
way that it looks like a wonderful and adventur-
ous fairy tale, but with the loss of its individual
genuineness, and even all the Abderite family
likeness.

Please to attend :—"The town of Abdera,"
says he, " was the most scandalous and impious
town in all Thracia, swarming with poisoners,
conspirators, murderers, libellers, pamphleteers,

and rioters. By daylight no one was sure of
his life, by night it was worse; and when the
scandal was at its height, the Andromeda of
Euripides was performed; it pleased all the
spectators, but the passage that produced the
greatest effect on the imagination was that
which the poet puts into the mouth of Perseus
—'O Cupid, prince of gods and men!'

"The following day all the people spoke only in
jingles, and of nothing else but the sentimental
monologue of Perseus—'O Cupid, prince of gods
and men!' To say the truth, this passage is the
only sentimental one, in the whole fragment of the
speech of Perseus, which has accidentally been
preserved, as our readers may see for themselves
by consulting the original. In every street of
Abdera, in every house, nothing but 'O Cupid!
Cupid!'—in every mouth, nothing else but 'O
Cupid, prince of gods and men!' The mania
spread, and all the town, like the heart of one
man, was open to love. No druggist could get
rid of an ounce of hellebore; no armourer had
the heart to make a weapon of death. Friendship and virtue met and kissed each other, and
hovered over Abdera. Every Abderite took
his shepherd's flute; every lady laid aside her

purple, and sat down chastely to listen to the song."

Really a very pretty chapter! All the youths and maidens found it delightful. "O Cupid! Cupid! prince of gods and men!" And thus a single verse of Euripides, and one the like of which the commonest street-singer might compose by scores, standing, as Horace says, on one leg, performed a wonder which could not be achieved by all the priests, prophets, and wise men of the world together, namely, the miracle of changing the scandalous, abominable, and impious town of Abdera into an innocent and lovely Arcadia! This, of course, pleases the sentimental male and female lovers and turtle-doves! It is only a pity, that in the whole history, as brother Yorick relates it, there is not a word of truth.

All the secret is, the wonderful man was in love when he imagined all this, and he wrote as it becomes every honest inamorato and virtuoso to do, who rides his own hobby-horse and fancies he writes the truth. Only it is not fair of him to accuse the poor Abderites of the worst crimes which can be charged against mankind, in order to pay a compliment to his favourite god

Cupid. Not one among the Greek and Roman antiquaries can rise and show that anything so bad could be said of this worthy people. They had, it is true, their humours and spleens, and, as we know, they had not a very large share of sense and reason; but to represent their town as a murderers' hole goes beyond the bounds of the widest poetical licence. This sort of liberty, like everything else in the world, however large a step you allow it, must have its limits.

Lucian of Samosata, in the preface to his celebrated little book, "How History should be Written if possible," tells the story quite otherwise, although (with his permission) not very justly either. He must have heard something of the King Archelaus, and the Andromeda, as well as the singular extravagance which overtook the Abderites, and how they were obliged to call to their aid Hippocrates, to put everything to rights in Abdera. And now see what a mess the author makes of the whole story. He says: —"The comedian, Archelaus, who was at that time the most eminent of the day," (a kind of Greek Garrick or Talma),—" this Archelaus came in the time of King Lysimachus to Abdera, and represented the Andromeda of Euripides. It was a fine summer's day; the sun blazed over the heads of the Abderites, which were, it is said, quite hot enough before. The whole town returned from the play with a fever. On the seventh day the illness ended with most of them by violent bleeding of the nose, or a strong perspiration; but a strange symptom remained, for when the fever subsided they were attacked with an irresistible propensity for speaking in iambics, declaiming tragic verses, and spouting, as they stood still, or moved about, entire tirades from the Andromeda, or singing the monologue of Perseus, ' O Cupid!'" &c.

Lucian, in his satirical way, is very merry about this idea. "How absurd it must have been to see all the streets of Abdera swarming with pale meagre creatures, worn out by a seven-days' fever, singing 'O Cupid, prince of gods and men!' with all their might!" He asserts, too, that this epidemic lasted till the return of the winter, which was an unusually cold one, put an end to it.

It must be conceded that Lucian's way of relating the circumstance is far preferable to Yorick's, because, singular as this Abderite fever may appear, all physicians will agree that it was at any rate possible, and all authors, that it was characteristic. It may be said of it as say the

Italians, "*Se non è vero, è ben trovato ;*" but *true* it is not, by any means, as may be found from the simple circumstance, that, at the time it was said to have occurred in Abdera, the place was uninhabited, the Abderites having emigrated several years before, leaving their town to the rats and frogs.

Briefly the circumstances were as we have related them, and if the paroxysm which befell the Abderites after the performance of the Andromeda is to be termed a fever, it was no more than that kind of dramatic fever of which we have seen so many instances in Italian and German towns at the present time: the evil was not in the blood, but in the Abderitanism of the good people in general.*

Meanwhile it cannot be denied, that in some cases, where the fire found more tinder and more fuel, the matter may have been serious enough to call for a physician's help, and this, probably, gave rise to Lucian's mistake, that all were afflicted with a kind of high fever together. Fortunately Hippocrates was in the neighbourhood,

---

* [England has been by no means free from such fevers, and America has had her share. Jenny Lind was the occasion of such an epidemic in both countries.— TRANSLATOR.]

and, as he pretty well knew the Abderitan constitution, a few pounds of hellebore set all speedily in its former state, so that the Abderites
ceased to sing "O Cupid, prince of gods and
men!" and became just as rational as they were
before.

END OF VOL. I.

Woodfall and Kinder, Printers, Angel Court, Skinner Street, London.